Sustaining the Fires of Revival

Turning God's Visitation Into a Habitation

Randy Colver

Sustaining the Fires of Revival

ISBN 978-0-615-66285-5

Contents

"If your Presence does not go with us,
do not send us up from here" (Ex. 33:15).

Foreword

Revival is right.

Revival is no longer an option for our country. Revival for the church in America has become survival in the tide of opposition.

I appreciate Randy Colver's insightful look into "Sustaining the Fires of Revival." He's asking the right questions about revival. Anyone who desires more of God and longs to see the church become the promised radiant bride will glean from the answers Randy's discovered.

His interviews with respected revival leaders of our time, many of whom are my good friends, add fire to the belief that anyone, anywhere, anytime can have a move of God.

You just have to be willing to pay the cost.

Yours for revival,

Steven J. Gray
World Revival Church
Kansas City, MO

Introduction

Why revival?

While writing this book, I received a phone call from my daughter, Tamara, who is a worship leader at a nearby church. She was deeply grieved to hear that another "Christian" song writer/artist had just revealed that she was a lesbian. I reminded her that every form of lust is sin and that every sin has consequences, terrible consequences, including the possibility of spiritual death.

With such sins becoming acceptable today, it seems that many Christians are expecting God to pour out fire and brimstone from heaven. A careful reading of the first chapters in Romans, however, reveals that when God turns people over to their sins, that is, in fact, the signal that His judgments have already begun. For when the Holy Spirit no longer restrains sin, sin's consequences have free reign.

Evidently, this artist saw herself as "being true to who she was." What she failed to see was that God was actually judging her by turning her over to her sin. Deception is the second sin to take up residence in a soul filled with lust—any lust, including homosexuality.

I then spoke to my daughter about hope—the *only* hope for this nation: *revival*. For years I've believed that revival is the answer to our nation's ills and I believe it now. What we need is God's holy fire to burn deeper and brighter than the passions that come from lust.

When lust burns unchecked, it will lead the sinner irrevocably to the unquenchable fires of hell. In contrast, God's love, fueled by the wood of Christ's cross, leads us to repentance and the purifying fire of God's holy presence. The former will consume us in eternal pain; the latter will burn in temporary, cathartic pain, making us stronger and purer by it. The result is holiness, an exquisitely beautiful thing (2 Chron. 20:21).

The media played up this artist's decision, but that shouldn't surprise us. The world flaunts those who rebel against God's Word, especially those who claim to be Christians.

In fact, it would not surprise me that the day will come when a book like this will be labeled as inciting hate or causing sedition. But true heroes are those who burn in holy anger against sin, who take courage and speak boldly for truth. They are those who are zealous for Him—zealous for revival.

In stark contrast to this young ladies defiance of God's Word, Amy Carmichael, a true hero of the Lord, once wrote:

Give me the love that leads the way,
The faith that nothing can dismay,
The hope no disappointments tire,
The passion that will burn like fire,
Let me sink to be a clod:
Make me Thy fuel, Flame of God.

This book is about fire—revival fire—and it is for those who want to become the fuel of God. But it is not just about revival; it is about *sustaining* revival, for a quick fix will not do. The flames of sin already run like a brush fire across this land. Unless we move quickly with sustained revival—to fight fire with fire—only a charred patch of ground will remain.

—The Author

1

The Fire of Revival

"I have come to send fire on the earth,
and how I wish it were already kindled!"[1]
—Jesus Christ, Son of God

What is revival?

To a Christian, pursuing Christ's presence stands out as one of the greatest longings of the heart. And few things capture the heart as much as moments of revival. Ask me if I remember last week's sermon or what I read two weeks ago, and I'll probably offer a wild guess. But ask me how I felt to be baptized with the Spirit over thirty years ago, or how I felt during a remarkable elder's retreat where His presence came in overwhelming joy, or how I trembled from His presence after awakening from a spiritual dream, and I'll recount to you in great detail—with deep, burning passion and longing—what His presence is like.

This is revival in its broadest sense—His quickening presence bringing life to something spiritually dry and lifeless. It is the return of the church from its backslidings (Finney),[2] a time of visitation of the Holy Spirit when He imparts new life (R. A. Torrey),[3] it is:

[1] Luke 12:49 NIV.
[2] Charles Finney, *Lectures on Revival*, (Albany: SAGE Software, 1995) 13.
[3] R. A. Torrey, cited in Frank Damazio, *Seasons of Revival*, (Portland: BT Publishing, 1996) 111.

> …Divine intervention in the normal course of spiritual things. It is God revealing Himself to man in awful holiness and irresistible power. It is such a manifest working of God that human personalities are overshadowed and human programs abandoned. It is man retiring into the background because God has taken the field."[4]

Revival is necessary because we are creatures prone to laziness and lacking discipline—because, as the theologians put it, we have a tendency to sin. It is our nature to stretch out in Ezekiel's valley like so many parched bones—void of God's breath—and quite content to lie there.

Until God stirs.

And the old bones rattle.

Until we recognize how far we have fallen into the deep pit of sin—damp and dark and cold and full of dead things—until we recognize the degree to which things have deteriorated and a real cry for holiness wells up to repentance—until the Spirit, who is holy, breathes on us.

When does revival happen?

In the life of every person there occur certain watershed moments that become turning points—critical events that forever change the shape of our thinking or actions.

The turning point might be *confrontational*—as the moment when Christ interrupted Saul of Tarsus on his way to persecute the saints at Damascus. Christ broke through his misguided zeal and awakened him to the truth of the gospel.

This event became the defining moment and commissioning of Paul. He later reflected, "I was not disobedient to the vision from heaven. First to those in Damascus, then to those in

[4] Arthur Wallis, *In the Day of Thy Power*, 20, cited in Winkie Pratney, *Revival, Its Principles and Personalities*, (Lafayette: Huntington House Publishers, 1994) 16.

Jerusalem and in all Judea, and to the Gentiles also, I preached that they should repent and turn to God and prove their repentance by their deeds" (Acts 26:19-20). For Paul there was no more compelling turning point than those moments sprawled out under heaven's glory.

The turning point might be *theological*—as the moment when, out of great desperation and longing for a release from his burdens of guilt, Martin Luther received his revelation from Romans 1:17 that God justifies us by faith. The words Luther wrote leap off the pages: "Here I felt that I was altogether born again and had entered paradise itself through open gates." The results of that revelation turned Luther's life and the Church upside down.

The turning point might be *pastoral*—as the moment when the Apostle John turned in response to the voice of a trumpet behind him and immediately collapsed before the vision of Christ. In this way John received the testimony of Christ to each of the seven churches of Asia Minor. And the future of each church depended on the correct response to His warnings and admonitions.

At each turning point, there was an encounter with Christ. Only His life serves as the standard by which our actions and thoughts must be measured. Only His grace provides the necessary empowerment to change for the better.

It is not Saul of Tarsus, the brilliant Jewish scholar and zealous religious leader, whom God commissions. It is not men of scholarship with academic accolades that people long to see. They don't come to admire the diploma on the wall or the graduation ring on the finger. If you haven't discovered it already, *people are attracted to the Church because they want an encounter with Christ*. It is the presence of Christ that makes all the difference.

Nor is it, like Luther, the pious, religious monk that God wants (though He takes us as we are), but Christ chooses the humble man of faith who can utterly rely on Him.

It is not the wealthy church that impresses Christ, but rather the one that possesses "gold refined in the fire" (Rev. 3:18). God is looking for the church that will "Wake up! Strengthen what remains and is about to die" (Rev. 3:2 NIV).

For all that revival is and brings, revival *happens* at God's point of turning us.

Sustaining the Fires of Revival

Unfortunately, much of the Church in America has a "reputation for being alive" (Rev. 3:1) but it is dead! We no longer come to church because we need an encounter with God; we come to church so we can feel good. Why do we need the conviction of the Holy Spirit? We can fix all our problems with counseling and twelve-step programs and psychopharmacology.

However, an honest appraisal of the Church, our society, and ourselves leaves us coming up far short of the mark. Interview some random people in the market place and ask them what they think of the Church. You will discover some pretty sobering descriptors: irrelevant, out of touch, and powerless. And they will be mostly right.

People are bored with Christianity and church so they are looking for passion elsewhere—often in the form of lewd entertainment, pornography, and drugs. "Self" is the god of this age. The words of Samuel Chadwick ring true:

> The world will never believe in a religion in which there is no power. A rationalized faith, a socialized church, and a moralized gospel may gain applause, but they awaken no conviction and win no converts.[5]

We have catered long enough to the consumer Christians floating from church to church looking for something better to meet their selfish desires. God isn't a handyman trying to fix your

---

[5] Cited in Leonard Ravenhill, *Revival God's Way* (Minneapolis: Bethany House Publishers, 1983) 79.

problems. He's a passionate, holy Lover—untamed and uncontainable.

Unfortunately, the typical response to the Church's powerless condition is to hold a few midweek services and bill it as a revival. Sadly, this "hit and run" tactic only temporarily satisfies people's thirst. Then it's back to business as usual.

This response lacks any lasting results because repentance never has time to do a deep work. Only after acknowledging our miserable state and confessing our spiritual poverty in ever deepening ways, will the Spirit of God move afresh in a *sustained* manner.

Even though moments of revival may come—sometimes even seasons of revival—only a *sustained* revival really brings lasting change. Sustained revival is the kind our forebears called spiritual awakenings—movements lasting years, sometimes a decade—that emptied the bars, filled the churches, and changed society.

However, moving from a series of short revival meetings to sustained revival is a big step for most churches, and may take years of prayer and logistical preparation. In fact, our church held the short meetings for years, annually inviting Frank Seamster,[6] a revivalist preacher, to come and host the meetings. These short meetings had both the positive effect of preparing hearts for a deeper move of God and the negative effect of conditioning the congregation for short-term revival.

However, before the last series was scheduled, I asked our pastor if he had ever considered inviting Frank to come for a series of extended meetings, perhaps even leaving the schedule open ended. He replied that he had already been considering it, as his heart is also for sustained revival. Since the leaders were in agreement with this approach, and since there was a spirit of

---

[6] Frank Seamster has been heavily involved in the "Corn Field Revival" in Kansas and regularly travels the country like the old Methodist "circuit riders" sacrificing everything to see revival come to God's Church. (See the Interviews section.)

expectancy in the congregation, we launched an open-ended series with Frank.

Please understand—the core of revival work lies uniquely in the purview of the evangelist's gifting. Pastors and teachers nurture the local church for revival, prophets awaken the church with God's fresh word, and apostles break new ground to launch new works from those who are awakened, but the evangelist stirs up the dry bones and leads the lost into the kingdom. Although there is certainly overlap of these five gift-ministries and each contributes to revival in its unique way, nevertheless, the evangelist lives for this.

Frank is your old-fashioned "fire and brimstone" revival preacher. We launched the revival and with rapid-fire preaching he peppered the congregation with a mixture of Scripture verses on repentance, glimpses of society's sin, passionate pleas for more of the presence of God, and principles necessary to continue revival. "I want to tap into something eternal…How many still watch X-rated movies? God doesn't blink at sin…Revival is survival for the Church!…God is the true Seeker, so be seeker sensitive to Him." We laughed and cried and repented for 88 days of extended revival meetings—an incredible outpouring of God's presence.

We should not despise such brief or repeated seasons of revival. I am reminded of Solomon Stoddard, grandfather of Jonathan Edwards, who led five brief seasons of revival as a minister in Northampton, New England. These became the precursor to the first Great Awakening in North America.

The Cost of Revival

Unfortunately, sustained revival comes with a cost: *everything*. At Elijah's prayer, fire came from heaven to burn up the wood, the stones, the sacrifice, the soil, all the water around it—everything. What a picture of revival! God passionately desires for His holy presence to consume the destructible and purify the indestructible. But it will scorch before it softens. It will blaze before it refines. It will never say "Enough!" (Prov.

30:16), for behind it lies the all-consuming presence of God.

Our little "great heart" church pursued God for those 88 days, but ran out of strength about a week before the actual meetings ended. Other factors probably contributed to its demise, but it seemed to me that the congregation had not turned outward enough to the lost in the community and had begun to lose their passion for a deeper work of God.

Charles Finney warned years ago in his *Lectures on Revival* that even during revival, "the Christian's heart is liable to get crusted over, and lose its exquisite relish for Divine things." Finney, who was instrumental in the late Second (1820-1840) and Third Great Awakenings (1857-1859) in North America, explained how we need to continually deepen our relationship with the Lord in order to sustain revival:

> Revivals decline, commonly, because it is found impossible to make Christians realize their guilt and dependence, so as to break down before God. It is important that ministers should understand this, and learn how to break down the Church, and break down themselves when they need it, or else Christians will soon become mechanical in their work, and lose their fervor and their power of prevailing with God. This was the process through which Peter passed, when he had denied the Savior, and by which breaking down, the Lord prepared him for the great work on the day of Pentecost.[7]

Unfortunately, the fact that revival costs everything is precisely why so many pastors are reluctant to seek sustained revival. They are not ignorant of the price you have to pay. It burdens the staff, exhausts the administrators, wears on the members, often drives contributors away, and frequently angers the board. It will attract all kinds of criticism from the community, even from the Church.

---

[7] Charles Finney, *Lectures on Revival*, Ages Digital Library, Version 5, 281. This is from Lecture 15, *Hindrances to Revival.*

Without revival, however, we will never move past the paltry church services that corral the Spirit into twenty-minute productions or offer alternative after-glow meetings where the Holy Spirit's gifts might be found in a corner room—clean and sanitized.

Pastors that run such churches are ubiquitous. Not long ago, for example, we invited a pastor from a non-charismatic denomination to our church to speak. He was awed by the move of God in the worship service, which continued for over an hour with prophetic words, prayers, exhortations, and song. Yet for all his amazement, his only comment afterwards was that you could never *sustain* that kind of service. How his expectations were limited by his ecclesiastical baggage!

Remember when the demoniac encountered Christ and our Lord drove the demons from him into the heard of pigs? Matthew recorded that "the whole town went out to meet Jesus." But immediately after they encountered Him, "they pleaded with him to leave the region" (Mt. 8:34). Imagine that! Jesus healed the demoniac and *they pleaded with him to leave their region.* Jesus had come among them and they wanted Him to leave! He does one mighty thing and that was enough for them.

We look on their actions with such contempt, but don't we do the same thing when we reject revival, or feel satisfied with our little time of refreshing? Doesn't our prayerlessness tell Him that He is unwanted? Don't we send Christ away by our sins?

Look again at the story of Moses when he turned aside to the bush that burned but was not consumed. As Moses drew near, God called to him from the flaming bush and said that the place he was standing was holy ground (Ex. 3:1-5). But how many pastors today would rather go on tending the sheep, rather than turn aside to the fire? Isn't God calling out to us from the fire? Isn't revival His way of getting our attention and drawing us to Himself?

For all of this, however, we must consider one other Person who may hold back revival. God Himself may choose to delay revival, even though His heart is ultimately in favor of it. He may withhold revival because the congregation may not be ready to make the sacrifice—spiritually, materially, logistically and physically. *Fire did not fall for Elijah on an empty altar*, and revival fire doesn't fall on an empty altar of sacrifice. If congregants are not willing to sacrifice their time, money and effort to support revival, it may never come. And true sacrifice is not giving of our abundance, but of our need. We are happy to give if we have extra things, or time, or money, but don't ask for something we need. That is too much to expect!

Each individual must determine before God what sacrifice needs to be made. But for most of us in the U.S., like me, the sacrifice will probably involve giving up some form of entertainment (e.g. swapping TV time for prayer time).

A Prescription for Revival

Do you want revival—*sustained* revival? If you do, then R. A. Torrey's simple prescription provides the way:

> I can give a prescription that will bring revival...Revival to any church, or community, or any city on earth. First: let Christians get thoroughly right with God. If this is not done, the rest will come to nothing. Second: let them bind themselves together to pray for revival until God opens the windows of heaven and comes down. Third: let them put themselves at the disposal of God for His will as He sees fit in winning others to Christ. That is all, I have given this prescription around the world...and in no instance has it failed. It cannot fail.

Like Elijah of old, the church must take a stand against the ungodliness of this world and call down the fire of God. Sustained revival is an intense, spiritual fire that burns deep and prolonged. "The god who answers by fire—he is God!" (1 Kings 18:24 NIV). To the heart crying out for God, He will answer by fire.

Revival Principles

1. Revival is God's quickening presence bringing life to something spiritually dry and lifeless.
2. Revival is necessary because we have a tendency to sin.
3. Fire doesn't fall on an empty altar. Similarly, revival fire doesn't fall on an empty altar of sacrifice.
4. Ever deepening repentance is necessary for sustained revival: the deeper the repentance, the deeper the revival.
5. You must be willing to commit everything to achieve sustained revival.

2

Prayers on the Altar of Fire

The fire must be kept burning on the altar continuously;
it must not go out.—Leviticus 6:13 NIV

Keeping the Fires Burning

Once, while teaching a Sunday morning class on the spiritual disciplines, I mentioned the revival at Herrnhut in Moravia in 1727.

You should have seen the blank stares.

I went on to explain that under the leadership of Count Zinzendorf, a rag-tag assortment of religious refugees gathered on his estate to seek sanctuary. Even though differences of background, languages, and faiths divided the community, Zinzendorf assembled a small group together to pray. Soon a revival broke out with such intensity that Zinzendorf remarked, "The whole place represented truly a visible habitation of God among men."

Just as the sacred fire was never permitted to go out on the tabernacle's altar (Lev. 6:13 NIV), so this community believed that the fires on the altar of prayer must burn incessantly to God. Remarkably, that tiny prayer meeting turned into a twenty-four hour vigil that lasted over one-hundred years!

Six months later, Count Zinzendorf challenged the community to begin sending and supporting missionaries to spread the gospel. Twenty-six immediately responded! From that point on, the Moravians carried out the largest missionary endeavor before the twentieth century.

This is *sustained* revival. And it is fueled by prayer.

When David called to the Lord in prayer, the Lord "answered him with fire from heaven on the altar" (1 Chron. 21:26 NIV). In the same way, a church that wants the fire of revival must build an altar of prayer. And a church that wants to sustain revival, must keep the fire burning on that altar.

Charles Finney recognized the necessity of continued prayer in revival:

> Unless I had the spirit of prayer I could do nothing. If even for a day or an hour I lost the spirit of grace and supplication, I found myself unable to preach with power and efficiency, or to win souls by personal conviction.[8]

Prayer was also the precursor to our recent mini-revival. Our pastor, Pete Mullins, had wisely steered the church to become a house of prayer. He dedicated Wednesday service completely to prayer and launched another early afternoon prayer meeting on Tuesdays.

The mid-week meeting is characterized by spontaneous prayers, new songs and other prophetic expressions blended together with worship. The Tuesday meeting follows an agenda from the Lord and centers on specific intercession. Remarkably, many come from different churches in the community to attend both meetings.

In addition to these, specific "prayer watches" are manned by small groups during the week. As these grow, the intention is to eventually provide prayer around the clock.

---

[8] Hugh P. Jeter, *Holy Spirit Conviction and Revival*, **Paraclete**, Winter 1972, 7-8. Cited in *America's Great Revivals*, Dimension Books (Minneapolis: Bethany Fellowship) 10.

Intercession

All of these intercessors work behind the scenes to hear God's heart and move his hand. In fact, most revivals are birthed and sustained by the groans of prayer warriors—many of them nameless intercessors.

Let me take a moment to illustrate this from the Welsh revival of the 1850's, where prayer and intercession prepared the way for God to move. Things actually started in Ireland, where a woman and four newly converted men prayed for three months in 1856 until they claimed their first conversion. Soon fifty gathered for prayer, and then a nationwide prayer movement assembled over 40,000 people to intercede for Scotland. All of this took place before Evan Roberts, the Welsh revivalist, carried the torch "the length and breadth of Wales."

Weeping and Groaning Intercession

Often during the Welsh revival, Evan Roberts would simply begin to pray and weep and the people would cry out to God. This could not have happened if the hot embers of intercession had not already been burning long before.[9]

The leaders of revival must embrace the need for "weeping intercession." In the Old Testament, the priests who ministered before the Lord were to "weep between the temple porch and the altar" (Joel 2:17).[10] This covered area in front of the temple was the place where the priests used to pray. We often think of a priest's duties as offering sacrifices and sprinkling blood, but the priests were also to represent the people, intercede for them, and hear God's heart.

Intercession that brings the burdens of the people before the throne of grace ultimately leads to weeping, for even Christ's intercession during His life on earth was characterized by "loud cries and tears" (He. 5:7 NIV) and He continues that same

[9] As a result of this revival, by early 1905 over 100,000 had converted.
[10] When we unite with the heart of Christ, His presence comes and brings conviction of sin (cf. Joel 2:12-13).

intercession in heaven for us (He. 7:24-25). When we unite with His heart through intercession, we will begin to weep for His people.

This also took place in the recent extended revival at Brownsville Assembly of God in Florida (1995-2000). Looking back at the videos of the service, it is not uncommon to see Pastor John Kilpatrick with his hands in his face weeping and praying during the altar call. In fact, during an interview in 2008 by Charisma magazine about the Lakeland revival, Kilpatrick sobbed on the phone as he recalled how the presence of God had "ruined" him at Brownsville.[11]

Recognizing the importance of this type of intercession, Evangelist Steve Hill published a book entitled, *Time to Weep: The Language of Tears*.[12] In it Hill described how our hearts must be broken in such a way that we weep for the sinful state of humankind and toward the lost souls of this world. Our tears provide the necessary moisture to soften fallow hearts for the planting of God's Word. The Psalmist declared, "He who goes out weeping, carrying seed to sow, will return with songs of joy, carrying sheaves with him" (Ps. 126:6 NIV).

I believe this perspective played an important and foundational role in preparing hearts for the outpouring at Brownsville, where Steve Hill was invited to bring convicting messages regularly during the revival.

Prayer and intercession also sparked the Pentecostal revival at Azusa Street in California led by William Seymour, a one-eyed, uneducated son of former slaves who simply believed God and prayed for revival.[13]

---

[11] See Paul Steven Ghiringhelli, *Lakeland Revival Intensifies*, Charisma Magazine, April, 2008. Accessed April 22, 2010; http://www.charismamag.com/index.php/news/19624.

[12] Stephen Hill, *Time to Weep: The Language of Tears*, (Together in the Harvest Publications: Foley, Alabama) 18.

[13] Today there are over 500 million Pentecostals and Charismatics who trace their spiritual lineage to Seymour.

Frank Bartleman, an eyewitness of the Azusa revival, wrote of the intercessory prayer that occurred prior to this remarkable move of the Spirit:

> A great burden and cry came in my heart for a mighty revival…Intercessors were the need…I found most Christians did not want to take on a burden of prayer. It was too hard on the flesh. I was carrying the burden now in ever increasing volume, night and day. The ministry was intense. It was the "fellowship of His sufferings," a "travail" of soul, with "groaning that could not be uttered" (See Rom. 8:26-27 NIV).[14]

The Welsh revival was a precursor to the Spirit's outbreak at Azusa. In fact, Frank Bartleman wrote to Evan Roberts personally, requesting that he pray for California. Roberts wrote back three times to encourage him, thus linking the two great revivals by prayer. "I feel their prayers had much to do with our final victory in California,"[15] wrote Bartleman.

The spirit of intercession continued throughout the early days of the Pentecostal revival. The newspaper of the Azusa Street Mission, *The Apostolic Faith*, recorded the following in the May, 1907, edition:

> Three days of fasting and prayer were set apart at the Mission for more power in the meetings. The Lord answered and souls were slain all about the altar the second night. We have felt an increase of power every night…The workers all got down before God and the power fell. This is the way of victory, to go down before God. The great need is prayer.

During this ten-day fast, a remarkable outpouring took place that included speaking in tongues and other charismatic phenomenon. Soon, full revival broke out and services were packed with over-flow crowds of "Azusa Pilgrims" seeking the Pentecostal experience.

---

[14] Robert Liardon, *Frank Bartleman's Azusa Street* (Shippensburg, Destiny Image, 2006) 16, 21.
[15] Ibid., 36.

The Apostolic Faith recorded numerous occasions of weeping and intercession during this revival, often for the lost or by those seeking the Baptism with the Holy Spirit. The testimony of one Mrs. W. H. Piper must have been characteristic of so many:

> I was now very hungry for the Baptism in the Holy Spirit. I began again to seek and again I began to weep. This time it did not seem as though I were [*sic*] weeping but rather that Christ was weeping through me. God was thus showing me the suffering and agony of Christ in the Garden of Gethsemane. I passed through the Garden experience with Christ, God letting me suffer all I could stand. I felt any more grief would kill me.
>
> The next night I wept with Christ all night over lost souls. [16]

[16] *The Apostolic Faith*, vol. 1, no. 10.

Prophetic Imagination

Not only do we find weeping intercession in this simple testimony, but also what I call the "prophetic imagination" aided her union with Christ's heart. She pictured Christ suffering in Gethsemane and, as a result, God's desire for the lost filled her heart.

Through a sanctified imagination, we can unite with Christ's current ministry of intercession in heaven. Heaven is open to us; we must simply avail ourselves of the opportunity to come before the throne of grace (He. 4:16).[17]

In contrast, one of the quickest ways to end revival is to fill the mind with base images. But when we pray while dwelling on biblically-inspired images, Christ is able to cause our intercession to soar into the heavenlies.

One way to do this is to picture yourself stepping through the door of heaven, bowing before His throne, and casting the crowns of your achievements before Him (Rev. 4:1-11). Gaze on the throne. Let His love envelop you and be silent as you hear His heart.

Here we find a key to intimate intercession and a key to sustaining revival: all those who desire revival must use the prophetic imagination to join the mind and spirit together in communion with Christ.

Incense and Fire from the Altar

In the Old Testament, God commanded the Israelite priests to offer "sweet incense" on the altar of incense in the Tabernacle of Moses (Lev. 4:7). The fragrant, holy aroma from this unique blend of spices (Ex. 30:34-38) must have filled the Holy Place—infusing the priest's garments and permeating the walls, thus bringing with

[17] See my books, *The Courtroom Ministry of Heaven* and *Lessons on the Charismata and the Ministry Gifts*, http://stores.lulu.com/drcolver.

it an indelible sensory pleasure few but God and priest ever enjoyed.

Once a year, on the Day of Atonement, the high priest carried a censor filled with this burning incense into the Most Holy Place—into the very presence of God. There it intermingled with the *Shekinah* cloud of God's glory.

From this we see how prayer and God's glory uniquely blend together, partly of earth and partly of heaven, bringing delight and pleasure to both. But oh, so few enjoy it!

David wrote: "May my prayer be set before you like incense..." (Psalm 141:2 NIV). And in John's revelation, the apostle saw the living creatures and elders in heaven, each "one had a harp and they were holding golden bowls full of incense, *which are the prayers of the saints*" (Rev. 5:8 NIV).

Something wonderful happens in our spirits when God's glory and our prayers intermingle. God delights in our prayers and we, in turn, delight in His glory. Soon the perfume of His presence fills us and delights others who bask in the glory that lingers long after we rise from our knees.

Christ's priestly intercession led Him to the cross, the finest act of intercession because it was done in totality for others. Our intercession must also follow this course—to offer ourselves in prayer for others. This results in "revival," but it is also at the center of life in Christ. For Christ continues in the way of the cross—the way of intercession—eternally in the heavenlies. By intercession, then, our lives mingle with His and share His ministry and glory.

Once, when a plague broke out against the Israelites for their rebellion, Aaron, the high priest and brother of Moses, ran into the midst of the people offering incense to make atonement for them. "He stood between the living and the dead, and the plague stopped" (Nu. 16:41-48 NIV).

Beyond the historical events recorded in Numbers, this story illustrates how the work of intercession is needed today. Sin has made extreme inroads into our world much like a plague. In our communities, our homes, and our individual lives, we have reaped the consequence of sin—*death*—the death of truth, the death of goodness, as well as natural and spiritual death.

Just as incense and fire from the altar rescued the people from the plague, in the same way, we must intercede to stop the plague of sin. With great urgency Aaron took the incense and ran between the living and the dead. So too, we must offer passionate prayers for revival—to petition God to come and rescue those bound by sin.

Intercession, like incense, creates a barrier between God's judgment and the people. Is it not for those who are plagued by sin? Is it not for the lost and the dying of this world?

When God says He could find no intercessors for Israel (Ezek. 22:30), it meant that no one stood in the gap; no one ran with the incense of prayer to stand against the spread of sin.

It is time for intercessors to run! Run between the living and the dead. Rescue those on the path to destruction and intercede to stay the hand of judgment.

Here again is a key to sustaining revival. Without the intercessors standing in the gap, without intercessors showing us the way to heaven marked out for us by our Pathfinder, Jesus Christ, revival will not continue. Just as the incense was to burn continually before the Lord, so our prayers for others must continue so that the fires of revival do not go out.

A Heart Aflame

Paul wrote, "through us spreads everywhere the fragrance of the knowledge of him" (2 Corinthians 2:14 NIV). Intimate passion for Christ diffuses a spiritual fragrance of the presence of the Lord upon all those for whom we come in contact. Like the broken bottle of perfume Mary poured out on the Lord's feet (Jn. 12:3), passionate hearts pour out an anointed fragrance of God's presence.

This passion comes from the hidden place of prayer. There God communes with our hearts and tells us of His love for us. There, in the quiet "secret garden" of His love, He romances and ravishes our hearts. There He makes Himself known in an intimate way. There He makes Himself known in a delightful way—more to be desired than any false passion of this world: "for your love is more delightful than wine" (Song 1:2 NIV).

Intimate passion for Christ comes from a heart aflame for God. A heart aflame is consumed by the Lord. "Take me away with you," is the cry of such a heart!

The Song of Solomon is not just a poetic love ode from Solomon to a shepherdess bride. It is a declaration in beautiful imagery of the extravagant passion between Christ and His Bride—the Church.

He longs to hear the voice of the Bride and describes it as "sweet" (Song 2:14). This is the heart of Christ to His Church. He longs for the intimate prayers that allow His love to be expressed. He whispers: "All beautiful you are…You have stolen my heart" (Song 4:7, 9 NIV).

"My lover spoke and said to me, 'Arise, my darling, my beautiful one, and come with me'" (Song 2:10). Christ bids us to come away. He calls us to the secret, private garden. This is a call to intimacy found in the private prayer life of every believer.

Although in the Song she is at first a garden locked up, where He cannot come and share the intimate fruit of her life, she begins to respond to Him and open her heart. Eventually, she allows her Lord to blow His Spirit on her life which, in turn, spreads the fragrance of His presence to others. Finally, she learns to lean on Him—totally dependent on His love (Song 8:5).

Fire on the Front Lines

The tenderness of our intimacy with Christ turns into a passion against His enemies. "The kingdom of heaven," said Christ, "has been forcefully advancing, and forceful men lay hold of it" (Mt. 11:12 NIV). These are the words of invasion and warfare, of seizing the domain of the enemy and releasing the kingdom of God on earth. These are the words of confrontation in a clash of kingdoms!

God has never lost His fervency; should we?

There is a need today for forceful men and women—ones who are filled with a holy anger against the forces of darkness. (Not the kind of force that fills people with rage toward their fellows, or the kind that leads men to batter women and abuse children.) This is a zeal for things of the kingdom that is willing to overturn the tables of lust and drive away the idols.

Is Satan under your feet? Has God crushed Him there? Or do you let him slither around your toes?

If a snake creeps its way into a crib and threatens the life of a baby, it is not time to reason with it, to play with it haphazardly, or to watch in frozen fear as it raises its head to strike. It is time to strike first! So it is time to strike decisively in the heavenlies and pursue the enemy till he is defeated! A snake has slithered into our Father's domain and it is the privilege of every Christian to smash its head!

It is time to call the Church to repentance. It is time to call the Church to revival.

Intercessors war on the front lines of the spiritual battle for revival. They anticipate attacks from the kingdom of darkness and deploy countermeasures in the heavenly realms when the enemy strikes.

The Tuesday prayer warriors are trained by Sharon Mullins and other leaders to "see the battle and the plan of the enemy and thwart it before any damage is done." To accomplish this, the leaders wait on the Lord for specific meeting prayer topics to defeat the enemy's agendas. They might pray to break off rejection, to take back the land, or to capture God's vision for the season. Often this is revealed prophetically. Here is one topic dated May 11, 2010:

> This is what I'm hearing: "When the fire comes, will you be ready for it? Don't say, 'Yes,' too quickly for it comes to burn up all that is not me—all your ways and thoughts—even your plans and dreams," says the Lord. "What remains will be as pure gold that has been tried in the fire…The transition has begun; the heat has been turned up in all areas, and I continue to call, 'Come closer; come closer.' The heat is there to do what I have intended it to do, so you can become what I've intended you to be," says the Lord.

Revival will always bring with it resistance from the kingdom of darkness. Intercessors must recognize the reality of spiritual warfare and stand against these forces. The lives of many are placed in their hands. If intercessors should give up, the revival cannot be sustained.

Revival Principles

1. "It is in the closet, with the door shut, that the sound of abundant revival will be first heard."—Andrew Murray[18]
2. Prayer keeps your spirit burning for God.
3. "Travail of soul is the only real revival prayer." —Charles Finney
4. All those who desire revival must use the prophetic imagination to join the mind and spirit together in communion with Christ.
5. If the prayers of intercessors are not offered continually before God, revival will neither break out, nor continue.

[18] Andrew Murray, *The Ministry of Intercession* (Kensington: Whitaker House 1982) 161.

3

The Fire of God's Word

"His word is in my heart like a fire,
a fire shut up in my bones."
—Jeremiah, Son of Hilkiah

Preaching Revival

Revival without the Word of God is no revival at all. But revival preaching consists not of feel-good positive thinking, or even of self-help steps for improving one's life. Revival preaching must be direct and confrontational.

Revival preaching must be full of the fire of God's Word: burning away the chaff, cleansing us from impurities, softening hardened hearts, warming us by His presence, glowing with the light of life, energizing us by the Spirit and setting the hearts of others on fire.

Unfortunately, most Christians would rather be coddled and told how good and wonderful they are! Our nation is full of churches that entertain us with performances and appease us with smiling preachers who promise the good life. And sermons are more often downloaded off the Internet than received from the heart of God.

Is it any wonder people leave church exactly as they came?

"If you leave people as you found them," Smith Wigglesworth said, "God is not speaking by you." If God is not speaking by us, what do we have to say?

Like Jeremiah, a revival preacher must carry the coals of God's word deep in the furnace of the spirit—"a fire shut up in my bones." Stoked by prayer and meditation, and fanned by the Spirit's breath, that word becomes an uncontainable inferno—it must be released. And when it is, that blazing word breaks forth to draw humankind to God, to conviction and to repentance. "I set myself on fire," said John Wesley, "and the people come to see me burn."

Where are the preachers who really hear from heaven what God says about their church? Christ still walks among all the candlesticks in heaven—each one representing a different church (Rev. 1-3 NIV) and the light it brings to the world. And He still sends His Word to correct the course of each church.

Are we *listening*? Has our light faded?

To one church Christ sent this edict: "Remember the height from which you have fallen! Repent and do the things you did at first" (Rev. 2:5 NIV). This Word is directional, deliberate, pointed, and decisive. It calls for radical change—like plucking out the offending eye or cutting off the offending hand.

God's Word is "like a hammer" said the prophet Jeremiah (Jer. 23:29). And it must be swung like one to break the hardened hearts of Christian and non-Christian alike. A hammer doesn't do its work sitting on the shelf or hiding in a drawer. "Hammering" God's Word means preaching with passion and conviction. It means striking with precision and driving sins away by the Holy Spirit.

God's Firebrands

A burning stick held by itself soon smolders out. But in the hands of God, it becomes a firebrand[19] to ignite the world.

George Whitefield lit the fires of the First Great Awakening[20] during his preaching tour in the colonies of America in 1739-40. He spoke with great pathos, tears, and zeal, born out of his own personal devotions. In fact, he preached with such fervency that he often lay breathless after his message.

One writer commented:

> "Few could withstand the sight. It woke up affections and touched the hidden springs of the heart as nothing else could ever do; men could not hate one who loved and wept for their souls."[21]

He attracted crowds of up to eight thousand people at a time, who "shut up their shops and forgot their secular business"[22] to hear him speak in the open air. His farewell sermon on the Boston Common drew 23,000 people from the surrounding area. Benjamin Franklin said his commanding voice could reach far more!

Not all revivalists spoke with the same emotion. Edwards and Finney often simply taught—Finney with the convincing arguments that characterized attorneys, Edwards often by reading his messages. But all spoke with power and intensity, fueled by the Spirit of Burning. And all spoke the gospel message of the Kingdom.

---

[19] Amos 4:11.

[20] The First Great Awakening lasted from 1725 to 1760.

[21] M. L. Loane, *Oxford and the Evangelical Succession* (London: Butterworth, 1950) 61. Cited in Marion Aldridge, *George Whitefield: The Necessary Interdependence of Preaching Style and Sermon Content to Effect Revival*, Journal of the Evangelical Theological Society, 23/1 March 1980, 61.

[22] J. Smith, "A sermon on the Character, Preaching, &c. of the Rev. Mr. Whitefield," in G. Whitefield, *Fifteen Sermons Preached on Various Important Subjects* (Glasgow: J & M Robertson, 1972) 22. Cited in Marion Aldridge, 60.

The Fire of the Gospel

Like Whitefield, the revivalist must preach to shine light on the hidden corners of the heart and uncover the sin lurking in the darkness. Charles Finney often wrote of how the minister must "annihilate every excuse of sinners," "tear away the last lie," "and make him feel that he is absolutely condemned before God."[23]

> Every sinner has some hiding place, some entrenchment, where he lingers. He is in possession of some darling LIE, with which he is quieting himself. Let the minister find it out, and get it away, either in the pulpit or in private, or the man will go to hell in his sins, and his blood will be found on the minister's skirts.[24]

In this we can be greatly aided by the charismata. God knows the deep-seated sins we refuse to relinquish. The gifts of prophecy, words of knowledge and the words of wisdom place us in connection with God's heart. To the person who uses these gifts by the Spirit, he or she can uncover the deceptions and point out the true needs of each individual.

Paul described such an occurrence in his epistle to the Corinthians:

> But if an unbeliever or someone who does not understand comes in while everybody is prophesying, he will be convinced by all that he is a sinner and will be judged by all, and the secrets of his heart will be laid bare. So he will fall down and worship God, exclaiming, "God is really among you!"[25]

Men hide things in their hearts—sinful things—and these evils must be laid bare. Paul described how an encounter with God brought revival. But it required someone using the gift of prophecy to bring that encounter. Someone had to hear what was on God's heart.

---

[23] Charles Finney, *Revival Lectures*, Ages Library, 205-206.
[24] Ibid., 199.
[25] 1 Cor. 14:24-25 NIV.

An emotional response that brings a person to his or her knees is not unusual during revival. In fact, it is quite common and should be expected. John Wesley observed similar responses under Whitefield's preaching:

> …no sooner had he begun…to invite all sinners to believe in Christ than four persons sunk down close to him, almost in the same moment. One of them lay without sense or motion. A second trembled exceedingly. The third had strong convulsions all over his body, but made no noise unless by groans. The fourth, equally convulsed, called upon God with strong cries and tears. From this time, I trust, we shall allow God to carry on His own work in the way that pleases Him.[26]

Jeremiah lamented that our sins are bound into a yoke (Lam. 1:14). If we could see with spiritual eyes, we would recognize that the unsaved walk around us bent over under the weight of each one's yoke of sin. Only the gracious news of Christ's redemption can break this yoke.

It Only Takes a Spark

Revival preaching not only entails preaching the gospel inside the local church building, but it must also include encouraging congregants to share the gospel with the lost in their communities. To deepen and continue, the revival must be carried outside the church walls. It is the responsibility of all those involved in the revival to share the gospel with others and spark revival outside the church.

To this end the evangelists must impart God's burden for the lost. Many evangelists see their duty finished after preaching the gospel to the church, but the ministry of the evangelist must also include leading the church members into the community to win souls. In fact, the ministry of an evangelist is incomplete without this impartation.

[26] Recorded in John Wesley's journal of July 1739.

To whom should we share the gospel? William Booth, who founded the Salvation Army, instructed his followers to preach to any and all. God is "not willing that any should perish" (2 Pt. 3:9), and we should preach and share the gospel with the same zeal for souls.

It was not uncommon for Whitefield to preach to crowds in the open, though frequently interrupted by the rabble. He was undaunted by their insults and always looked them "in the face," confident of the gospel message.

In addition to the ministry of the evangelist, intercessors must pray for God's grace to turn the revival outward. Like Peter and John, they must petition the court of heaven for boldness and courage: "Now, Lord, consider their threats and enable your servants to speak your word with great boldness" (Acts 4:29 NIV).

Be forewarned; in this effort the Christian will find the greatest resistance to God's work.

Revival Principles

1. God's hammer will either drive you to your knees or drive you away.
2. "Plough until God changes their hearts."—Frank Seamster
3. "Do you see, do you see
   All the people sinking down?
   Don't you care, don't you care?
   Are you gonna let them drown?"
   —Keith Green, *Asleep in the Light*

4

When Revival Fire Falls

Oh, that you would rend the heavens and come down,
that the mountains would tremble before you!
As when fire sets twigs ablaze and causes water to boil,
come down to make your name known to your enemies
and cause the nations to quake before you![27]
—Isaiah, Son of Amoz

What Happens When Revival Comes?

Have you ever been in an earthquake? I have. I was ten years old in Anchorage, Alaska, when the Good Friday earthquake of 1964 literally shook the city apart. I was standing in our living room when a low, rumbling sound accompanied the violent shaking of everything—books and dishes falling from cabinets, swag lamps swaying, the TV falling on its face, the refrigerator door opening and bottles smashing on the kitchen floor, and the ground moving back and forth under my feet. My world changed—suddenly, surreally, overwhelmingly, completely. I was immediately thrown to the ground, helpless. My father had to pick me up and carry me outside!

That's what Isaiah says happens when God comes.

God comes to shake everything loose so that only His precious things remain. He has to burn up all the useless brushwood of our lives and boil up a new passion for Him. He has

[27] Isaiah 64:1-2 NIV.

to be glorified and His name praised. Simply put, our world has to come apart before God puts it back together again for His purpose and glory. And, I might add, until we are on the ground helpless, He won't come to rescue us.

Conviction and Repentance

How does God break us? All it takes is an encounter with His presence. Do you remember the story of Peter and the miraculous catch of fish (Luke 5:1-11)? The story goes something like this. Peter and his fisherman friends had worked all night and had caught nothing. But Christ told them to try again. When they let down their nets, they pulled in so many fish that the nets strained to hold the catch!

That's when Peter's world turned upside down.

He had come face to face with divine power—and it convicted him deeply. "When Simon Peter saw this, he fell at Jesus' knees and said, "Go away from me, Lord; I am a sinful man!" (Lk. 5:8 NIV). Peter's encounter with the power of Christ brought an immediate awareness of his own sinfulness.

Such an encounter is the beginning of revival. Whenever we draw near to God, whenever His presence comes in power, we gain an immediate and simultaneous revelation of God's holiness and our sinfulness.

Further, where God invades—where His kingdom comes—sin is repelled. Like the statue of Dagon that fell into pieces before the Ark of the Covenant, all the idols of this world must fall before His presence.[28] This is the clearest mark of revival.

"The fountains of sin need to be broken up," wrote Charles Finney. "In a true revival, Christians are always brought under such conviction; they see their sins in such a light that often they

[28] 1 Samuel 5:1-5.

find it impossible to maintain a hope of their acceptance with God."[29]

Hosea called it breaking up the "unplowed ground" (Hosea 10:12) and Finney echoed his words:

> Sometimes your hearts get matted down, hard and dry, till there is no such thing as getting fruit from them till they are broken up, and mellowed down, and fitted to receive the Word. It is this softening of the heart, so as to make it feel the truth, which the prophet calls breaking up your fallow ground.[30]

Conviction of sin was fundamental to the revivals that followed Finney's ministry and he employed several techniques to make sure that repentance was real and heartfelt. He was the first to use the "anxious bench" or prayer altar as we call it today. He often preached about sin and its consequences until the audience longed for deliverance. He would then invite them to another meeting where he would show them the solution to their deep need: salvation in Christ. This resulted in lasting conversions.[31]

Let me illustrate the conviction of sin that followed wherever Finney went. Once, after a revival meeting, Finney happened to visit a nearby factory. While he toured the place, a woman recognized him and spoke a derogatory remark. Finney, who was still full of the Spirit, responded only with a look of deep sorrow and compassion for her.

The lady was so convicted that she stopped working, sat down where she was and wept. Conviction of sin soon spread throughout the factory and the proprietor was forced to stop all the work and hold a prayer meeting. Within a few days the owner and nearly all the employees (about 3,000) were saved.

Finney explained, "A revival is nothing else than a new beginning of obedience to God. Just as in the case of a converted sinner, the first step is a deep repentance, a breaking down of heart,

---

29 Finney, 13.

30 Ibid., 34.

31 Perhaps over 250,000 converted to Christ through his ministry.

a getting down into the dust before God, with deep humility, and a forsaking of sin."[32]

Jonathan Edwards, a great prayer warrior and one of the greatest theologians that America has ever produced, witnessed many responses of brokenness during the First Great Awakening. As he read his sermons, his congregation became so distressed at their sinful condition that many wept uncontrollably.

Edwards properly understood that an emotional response to God lies at the heart of our relationship to Him. As he put it, "True religion, in great part, consists in holy affections."

Edwards also understood humankind's sinfulness, teaching that acts of rebellion against an *eternal* God deserve *eternal* consequences. His famous sermon, "Sinners in the Hands of an Angry God," was not only a warning of impending damnation to those who sin, but also a deliberate attempt to stir their emotions to repentance.

Confession and Repentance

Confession also plays a necessary part in revival and must be penetrating, specific, and heart-felt. Evan Roberts brought a simple message of confession and repentance:

1. Confess any known sin to God and put any wrong done to others right.
2. Put away any doubtful habit.
3. Obey the Spirit promptly.
4. Confess your faith in Christ publicly.

Unfortunately, most believers are too secretive about their sins and unwilling to expose them to God's light. But we must cry out like David: "Search me, O God, and know my heart; test me and know my anxious thoughts. See if there is any offensive way in me, and lead me in the way everlasting" (Ps. 139:23-24 NIV).

---

[32] Ibid., 14.

The words of David's prayer are not the empty, religious words that characterize so much confession today! David recognized the power of God and was ready and willing to let the fire of the Spirit refine him. He appropriated the three components of God's refining process: *conviction*, *confession*, and *repentance*.

Do you know how metal is refined? One of the things I vividly remember as a young boy was the awful odor of copper being smelted at the copper plant where my family lived in Arizona. The pungent odor of sulfur wafted from the plant stacks across the school yard and into our classroom. It didn't make recess all that pleasant and holding your nose didn't help.

To wrest the metal from the blue and green-colored rock, the ore had to be crushed and then burned at intense temperatures. This separated the impurities from the copper metal. After it was refined, a little train would chug out from the plant carrying the dross from the smelting process, make its way down the track, tip a special holding car, and dump the sludge out. Dark, black, smoldering ooze poured out.

When I ponder the Refiner's fire, I often think back to those days. It reminds me of the ugly sin God has to purge from our lives through the fire of conviction, confession and repentance—and sometimes through the intense heat of great trial.

Egypt was the "iron smelting furnace" for the people of Israel (Is. 48:10 NIV) and the trials in the wilderness purified the nation. But over the years their success and prosperity in the Promised Land slowed the refining process and the sludge of sin grew to an overwhelming amount. In fact, God viewed His people as the very dross left in the furnace:

> Then the word of the LORD came to me: "Son of man, the house of Israel has become dross to me; all of them are the copper, tin, iron and lead left inside a furnace. They are but the dross of silver…so will I gather you in my anger and my wrath and put you inside the city and melt you…As silver is melted in a furnace, so you will be melted inside her, and you will know that I the

> LORD have poured out my wrath upon you'" (Ezek. 22:17-22 NIV).

It is vitally important that the dross of sin be removed from our lives through God's refining process. Otherwise it overcomes us and we are fit to be treated like the dross we have become.

Sin blocks a heart from being broken, compassionate, and repentant. Worldliness dulls sensitivity to the Lord. No revival comes without moral transformation. And moral transformation does not come without conviction, confession and repentance. When repeated, this tripartite cycle forms the basis of sustaining revival.

That little train didn't stop at one trip. It kept going back and forth. As long as that smelting plant remained open, the sludge kept coming. As long as these three tools of God's refining process work in the believer's lives, revival continues.

"But who can endure the day of his coming? Who can stand when he appears? For he will be like a refiner's fire…" (Mal. 3:2 NIV). When God comes, He comes to refine us.

Aflame for Souls

Revival also brings a burning desire in the hearts of Christians for a harvest of souls. Finney wrote:

> They will feel grieved that others do not love God, when they love Him so much. And they will set themselves feelingly to persuade their neighbors to give Him their hearts. So their love to men will be renewed. They will be filled with a tender and burning love for souls. They will have a longing desire for the salvation of the whole world. They will be in an agony for individuals whom they want to have saved—their friends, relations, enemies. They will not only be urging them to give their hearts to God, but they will carry them to God in the arms of faith, and with strong crying and tears beseech God to have mercy on them, and save their souls from endless burnings.[33]

Jonathan Edwards kept a detailed record of the First Great Awakening in his *Faithful Narrative of the Surprising Work of God*, noting hundreds of salvations in different towns. Edwards wrote: "There was scarcely a single person in the town, either old or young that was left uncovered about the great things of the eternal world…souls did, as it were, come by flocks to Jesus Christ."[34]

Leonard Ravenhill, a modern-day revivalist, explained: "Evangelism is that revived Church's going to a world dead in sin and, under divine power, pulling down strongholds of Satan."[35]

When true revival takes place, the unsaved will affirm it, repent, and be saved! "The worst of human beings are softened and reclaimed, and made to appear as lovely specimens of the beauty of holiness."[36]

A World Aflame

In the days of the early Church, the disciples "turned the world upside down" with their witnessing. At Ephesus the city destroyed valuable occult items (Acts 19:18-19). In past revivals, such social sins as slavery and child labor were ended. The temperance movement, women's suffrage, and medical aid for the sick are just a few of the results of revival in this nation. During the Welsh revival whole communities came to the Lord. They even noted a sixty percent decrease in drunkenness.

Leonard Ravenhill noted that any "true revival can be proven by the fact that it changed the moral climate of an area or a nation."[37] The Great Awakenings broke out against the rising tide of rationalism. God launched the Pentecostal/Charismatic

[33] Ibid.
[34] Jonathan Edwards, *Works of Jonathan Edwards*, (Yale University Press, 1959). Cited in Pratney, 32.
[35] Leonard Ravenhill, *Revival God's Way* (Minneapolis: Bethany House, 1983) 63.
[36] Finney, 14-15.
[37] Ravenhill, 63.

movement at the turn of the twentieth century partly to counter the spread of humanism. True revival begins with repentance from personal sins, and ends with a society repenting from social sins.

It is also not uncommon for miracles, signs and wonders to occur during revivals. The foremost leaders of the healing revival in the U.S. in the 1950's, William Branham and Oral Roberts, operated in the gifts of healing. Branham used words of knowledge by the visitation of an angel to identify sicknesses. He felt vibrations in his left hand as he detected diseases. Roberts detected the presence of demons through his right hand. In a sense, we could say that in them operated the right and left hands of God for this revival.[38]

A Flame that Never Goes Out

Finally, the Church must be prepared to disciple souls that are saved during revival. To this and the gift ministries we turn in the next chapter.

Revival Principles

1. What marks revival, sustains revival.
2. "If God is talking, something is being shaken." —Frank Seamster
3. Only broken things are useful to God.
4. No revival comes without moral transformation.
5. The tripartite cycle of conviction, confession and repentance form the basis of sustaining revival.

---

[38] See Reg G. Hanson, "Wm. Branham Attends Roberts Campaign in Tampa, Florida," *Healing Waters* (March 1949) 6. Cited in David Harrell, Jr., *All things Are Possible: The Healing and Charismatic Revivals in Modern America*, (Bloomington: Indiana University Press, 1975) 36.

5

Sustaining the Fire of Revival through the Gift Ministries

"God does not send revival to a church; He does not send revival to a denomination; *He sends it to a man.*"
—John Kilpatrick

The Gifts God Uses

For all the history of revivals available to us and all the analysis of revivals historians provide, little, if any, covers the subject of the five-fold ministries (listed by Paul in Ephesians 4:11)[39] and their impact on revivals. Indeed, the important role of the individual's calling as apostle, prophet, evangelist, pastor or teacher is often overlooked or only briefly mentioned as part of a person's title. But a quick glance at revival history reveals the impact of these necessary gifts in revival, especially that of the evangelist.

George Whitefield, Maria Woodworth-Etter, Evan Roberts, Stephen Jeffreys, Smith Wigglesworth, Charles Price, Aimee Semple McPherson, Oral Roberts, William Branham, Billy Graham, Benny Hinn, and Steve Hill (just to name a few) were—or are—evangelists. And many, such as John Wesley and Charles Finney, were heavily evangelistic in their ministries as

---

[39] For an explanation of the five gift-ministries, see my book, *Lessons on the Charismata and the Ministry Gifts*, self-published online by Lulu.

well, depending on the occasion, though that may not have been their foremost gifting.

Revivals lie uniquely in the purview of the evangelist. And although all Christians may win souls and pray for revival, the evangelist stokes the fires of revival.

Even so, God used the other gift-ministries to bring revival as well. Jonathan Edwards, for instance, was clearly a teacher, though he discharged that office primarily as a pastor. If small pox had not tragically cut short his life, he might have been one of our most distinguished college presidents. Nevertheless, he was used mightily to break up the fallow ground at North Hampton, sparking revivals and preparing the way for the First Great Awakening in New England.

Similarly, Finney was evangelistic, but also a deep thinker and teacher. He, like Edwards before him, eventually moved into his role as a teacher—Edwards at Yale and Princeton; Finney at Oberlin College, where he continued until his death in 1875.

When the Flame Is Lacking

Finney understood that converts need to be grounded in the Word of God—the purview of the pastor and teacher. Winning souls is a first step, but making disciples is the imperative of Christ's commission in Matthew 28:19-20.

Here we observe that the deficiencies of any one revival often trace back to the lack of one or several of these gift-ministries. The evangelist often sparks revival, but not always are the newly converted gathered by the shepherds, or receive in-depth training by the teacher. George Whitefield complained about the backslidden not long after his last revival journey in New England. John Wesley recorded:

> But the last journey he made, he acknowledged to some of his friends, that he had much sorrow and heaviness in his heart, on account of multitudes who for a time ran well, but afterwards "drew back unto perdition."

> Indeed, in a few years, the far greater part of those who had once "received the word with joy," yea, had "escaped the corruption that is in the world," were "entangled again and overcome." Some were like those who received the seed on stony ground, which "in time of temptation withered away." Others were like those who "received it among thorns: "the thorns" soon "sprang up, and choked it." Insomuch that he found exceeding few who "brought forth fruit to perfection." A vast majority had entirely "turned back from the holy commandment delivered to them."
>
> And what wonder! for it was a true saying, which was common in the ancient Church, "The soul and the body make a man; and the spirit and discipline make a Christian." But those who were more or less affected by Mr. Whitefield's preaching had no discipline at all. They had no shadow of discipline; nothing of the kind. They were formed into no societies: They had no Christian connection with each other, nor were ever taught to watch over each other's souls. So that if any fell into lukewarmness, or even into sin, he had none to lift him up: He might fall lower and lower, yea, into hell, if he would, for who regarded it?[40]

John Wesley, who primarily walked in the apostolic gift, methodically gathered the newly saved into small "societies" for accountability and Bible training. Can we not clearly see how each gift-ministry plays a vital role in God's revival work?

Unlike many evangelists of his day, Billy Graham endeared pastors by connecting the saved from his crusades to local churches for pastoral care and teaching. Unfortunately, the pastor's vision is often on the local church and cannot comprehend or properly release the contribution of the mobile ministries. Most evangelistic ministries become "para-church" and take up the ministry vacuum outside the covering of a local church.

---

[40] John Wesley, *The Late Work of God in North America*, in *Sermons on Several Occasions* (Oak Harbor: Logos Research Systems).

Problems also result when one gift-ministry oversteps into another gift-ministry too far. We see an example of this in Oral Robert's "prophetic" proclamation that God would take him home if certain funds weren't raised. Or by Benny Hinn who once described the Trinity in less than respectable theology. (One should not try to be all the gifts.)

Though there certainly were exceptions, the Pentecostal movement as a whole was not known for its scholarship. In fact, except for a number of Bible colleges, the Pentecostal/Charismatic movement lacked the gift-ministry of the teacher for many years until we find Oral Robert founding his university, and Pat Robertson doing the same.

God further strengthened the teaching gift in the 1970s in response to the general lack of doctrinal stability among many Charismatics. He did this through the union of four teachers and a pastor in the Christian Growth Ministries in Fort Lauderdale, Florida. Though bringing balance to many through discipline and excellent teaching, even this group lacked the balance that all five ministries provide. As a result, discipleship became, in many places, authoritarian.

In many ways, you could characterize the Pentecostal/Charismatic movement as never quite finding a balance for all the gift-ministries. Coming close to God's best was the outpouring at Brownsville. Here we saw three gift-ministries moving remarkably well together: Evangelist Steve Hill, Pastor John Kilpatrick, and Teacher Michael Brown. But missing were equivalent levels of ministry from the prophet and apostle.

Releasing the Fire

Revival often lays dormant until a gift-ministry is released. Take Oral Roberts, for example. He wrestled "with a deep sense of discontent"[41] and felt entirely out of place as the pastor of a

[41] Oral Roberts, *The Call: An Autobiography* (Garden City: Doubleday, 1972) 37.

Pentecostal Holiness church, until he took the bold step to move out as an evangelist.

Rare is a person who can blend several of the gifts together well. John Wesley perhaps carried the mantle of apostle, teacher and evangelist in equal amounts. He wrote volumes, preached in the streets, and founded hundreds of churches. But few have these abilities so blended that a revival commences and is sustained by them. If we have learned anything, it is that the rugged individualist cannot sustain revival. We need each other's gifts.

Unfortunately, most church leaders only recognize one gift—the pastor—and shy away from the others. But I submit that sustaining the fires of revival requires the contribution of all the ministries.

Interviews

6

Frank & Naphtali Seamster

Modern-Day Circuit Riders
June 23, 2010

Frank and Naphtali Seamster are modern-day circuit riders who travel across the country to keep the fires of revival burning. Frank grew up traveling with his father to many revivals during the outpouring of the forties and fifties in North Carolina. Frank and Naphtali were instrumental in sparking the Cornfield Revival, now in Kansas City.

The Seamsters had parked their modest "fifth wheel" home behind our church in Newnan, Georgia, on July 23, 2010, and graciously allowed me to come and interview them. We sat down in their peaceful living room and you could immediately sense the presence of God as they shared.

Few are as dedicated to the Lord's work as Frank and Naphtali. And although I enjoyed Frank's stories and comments, it was Naphtali's comment that struck me the most about revival: You "don't get 'burned out' because the fire is burning for the right purpose."

ᘓ ᘐ

The Interview

R. What have you seen during your journeys about the Church and revival?

Frank. I agree that the only hope for our nation is revival.

Naphtali. —even the world.

F. Yes, basically, the terrible condition of our world and nation is the result of the Church's failure to be the Church. To be honest, we don't have a *prophetic* Church, but a *pathetic* Church. We need the power of God to be released in the Church—to be restored. If we don't have this, then it's over with.

R. Have you noticed anything in your travels that is vitally important?

N. Even though many members of the Church feel they are really running after God. In fact, even in the "prophetic" Church many are sinning because they have to express "my self." They are saying, "I've got to express what God is saying to me." They think they are moving toward revival, but the emphasis is still on them and not on Christ.

Then you have the rest who are still going to Church as though they are punching a clock. They are thinking, "God must be pleased with me because I go to church every Sunday." But they leave the church with their agenda. They get offended if the service goes too long. They want to get out so they can do what they want to do. The Church has become very self-centered.

Preaching has become very motivational—to try to inspire people—rather than getting people to do what the Bible says. To me, revival is living the Bible. It's getting back to what we're supposed to be doing: *raising the dead to prepare them to die*. Jesus said, "If any man will come after me, he will take up his cross and deny himself and follow me." Not a microphone, but the cross.

F. Because it has become such a motivational thing, there is no conviction—no preaching that brings conviction. Consequently, because there is no "from the gut" repentance, there is no permanent change. I was just telling some friends that I grew up in the eastern part of North Carolina, and, back in the forties and fifties, I remember my uncle coming to town—he was a tent preacher—an uneducated alcoholic—and just over night God saved and delivered him.

My dad was a part of that team, leading worship and preaching in the afternoon. The meetings were so full that the police were directing traffic 10 miles out to help people get to the services. Unfortunately, we have gotten so high-tech. But he would talk about what God had done to him and the alcoholics would come in and run to the altars, crying under powerful conviction. They would be instantaneously delivered.

We have such high-tech equipment, but where is the conviction? There is not a lot of conviction in the preaching. I believe that one of the greatest heresies in the Church today is the typical call to salvation: "come and repeat after me and now your saved." But you see no change in their lifestyle. But because they have repeated the sinner's prayer, they think they are saved.

We were just in a little town in North Carolina, where my uncle, Rubin Jones, held a big crusade. Six churches were established out of this crusade. I travel there to visit the grandson of Rubin Jones, who now owns the lumber company. The company was called Williams Lumber Company back then and years ago they had a man working there by the name of Howard Lunsford. Howard was the town drunk. He came one night during those meetings and before the message even concluded, he ran to the altar to be saved.

So powerful was his transformation in this small community and lumber company, that when they began to build the church, this lumber company brought the entire load of lumber and marked it, "paid in full." The owner explained, "If the God you are preaching about in this place can change Howard Lunsford's life, then we want to be a part of it."

R. Was this a part of how you became an evangelist?

F. That was part of it—a part of what I saw growing up. Of course, my dad would travel to all parts of eastern North Carolina as a part-time preacher. He worked in the cotton mill and they would get off in the afternoon and travel to different cities with Rubin Jones. In fact, at that time, my uncle was actually drawing larger crowds than Oral Roberts. I saw all this while growing up in a pastor's home.

At first, I didn't want to be a preacher, but when I finally said "yes" to God's call over thirty years ago, those visions of God's presence were the cry of my heart. That was what I wanted to see God do. They motivated me to want to see what God *could* do—revivals that were never less than two weeks long—where it took one week just to get a church ready for revival. Then you would see the second, third and fourth weeks really bring in the harvest. That was when the sinners came. When there was such an outpouring of the presence of God, that that's what drew the people—lives changed instantaneously.

I know there are different styles and methods of preaching, but it was back to the basics in those years. That's one of the reasons I don't believe we've even seen a measure of how God really moved back then. I don't believe we've tasted this again as a Church, because if we did, we could never go back. We have fads today, but we don't see hundreds and hundreds of people's lives change in one locale.

Also, one of the things we see in these past revivals is that their messages were not compromised. They preached on sin. And they preached in such a way that it brought conviction. Today, we don't hear much preaching on sin. We only hear about how God loves us. (Hey, that's an established thing. I don't need to hear that God loves me. I can see that in the New Testament.) Consequently, people don't think they do anything that's sin. They think, "What do I need to be convicted of?" *But if there is no conviction, there is no power.*

I think that one of the things that brings revival is repentance. And prayer is a key. That's the preparation. There would be days of prayer preparation—nights of just coming to church. And it was not prayer about Aunt Susie's big toe, but rather about hearts opening and people's lives changing. Also, they would pray for the meetings. Even though people had hard jobs—farmers coming in straight from the fields to pray—and fasting was a big part of it. And God moved. God did things. I believe it was because of prayer and fasting.

N. Today, in the church, people feel self-conscious and inhibited to go to the altar to repent and pray. But the altar should be our home—our life is to be an altar where our lives are poured out to him. We say, "Whatever you want, Lord." You didn't think about it; you just went to the altar.

F. It was not unusual to see people literally laying before the altars and crying out. The power, presence, and conviction of God—even during the message people were running to the altars.

I think one key that is missing today is that the people would not get up until they got their breakthrough. But today most people who come to the altar will stand. But there is something about kneeling before the altar—humbling yourself. Brokenness is so lacking today. But humility speaks to God. People used to tarry before God.

R. Are these things happening anywhere today?

F. In a few places, a few places. There is something that is happening, but not to the degree that we must have it if we are really going to see revival come to our nation. And it has to come to the Church first.

R. Would you say, then, that the lack of preaching on sin, the lack of humility, and the lack of conviction have prevented revival from really taking hold?

F. Yes.

N. I was thinking of a song written by a friend of ours. The name of the song is "Freedom." A lot of people in the Church think that freedom is jumping, dancing or raising our hands in worship. But these lyrics caught my attention, "mold me, make me, mend me, break me." That's what freedom is to me—freedom to choose Him.

F. While it may be true that freedom involves worship, it's much more than that.

N. There is so much more. It's freedom to die to Christ. What is our life in light of eternity? I recently read a statement by Billy Sunday, who was commenting on the Lord's Prayer: "Thy kingdom come, Thy will be done." He said that if we really wanted to do the will of God, we would do the will of God if it took every drop of blood in our body to do it.

F. He really preached with conviction.

N. He reached a hundred million people without a radio, without television, and without a loudspeaker. I really like little sayings like this that capture the heart of what God is trying to breathe on us. And I'm reminded of another quote from several hundred years ago by William the Third, Prince of Orange—somewhere in Old England. He said, "One sure way I will never see the ruin of my country: I will die in the last ditch." Meaning, you give your all and you gain everything.

F. Yet we want to gain everything and give nothing. And that is really why, as a whole, the Church is really powerless. It is really powerless—compared to the degree in which God wants it to powerful—compared to the Early Church. I think it is because there is no conviction. It's compromise. It's counting nickels. It's a corporation.

I am totally convinced that people really don't know the difference between right and wrong because it's not being preached. Like I said earlier, they just come and "repeat this prayer after me" and they're pronounced saved. "You're alright. You're ok." But the truth is that they are not alright; they are not ok. And the proof of that is in their life, and their lifestyle. Nobody preaches standards anymore.

So now there is no difference between the Church and the world. When you look at Mark 11, where Jesus cleansed the temple, it had nothing to do with selling tapes in the foyer; it had everything to do with the fact that He saw no difference between what was happening on the outside and what was happening in the temple.

N. In the established Church.

F. It was the same. There was no distinction—the same criticisms, backbiting, selfishness—the same sins. That's why He cleaned house. And if He came today, He would do the same thing. And He would start in the pulpit.

N. Then the choir, the worship team, the organist—all the leaders.

R. How long have you been doing this—traveling and preaching?

F. Well, I pastored and then traveled—all told about 25 years.

R. When a revival is launched correctly and you've prepared the church and they've been praying and repenting, what sustains the revival? And related to that, what causes it to end?

F. I would say that the thing that sustains revival is that you keep doing the same things that got it to where it's at. What causes it to end is that you quit—you stop doing the things that brought it to the place where you were really changing lives.

R. Do people get emotionally exhausted by it? Do they think they have repented deep enough?

N. I don't think so. Those who are totally serious about revival, they see themselves—even if they are not leaders—they see revival as so important that they set aside their agendas—I mean they have their own personal responsibilities, as we all do—but nothing trumps what God is calling them to do at the moment.

That doesn't mean you become religious about it. God gives us wisdom about our personal lives, too. But they don't get "burned out" because the fire is burning for the right purpose.

It's not about pushing themselves forward. And it's not about working for God; it's about working with God. Like it says in Matthew, we are yoked with Him and His yoke is easy, so you don't get run down. It's not a matter of saying, "I've repented of everything I can repent of." Rather, you concentrate on those who are coming in—to bring them into the place of freedom you are in.

If that means that I still need to continually go to the altar and repent, well, Paul said that we die daily. There is something in me that still needs to be repented of. If not, then I think we'd be like Enoch and God would just take us to be with Him. However, when we're still walking along the aisles of Wall Mart and our shadows aren't healing people, then there must be some place in God that I still haven't reached.

R. Is there a point in revival that people begin to reach out in the community?

N. To me the word itself will get out. When there's a fire, people want to come and take a closer look. It's not so much a program to go into the neighborhood; it's that neighbors see that your life has changed. They see boldness in you; they see cleanliness in you, and purity in you. Then they are drawn to it.

R. Yes. John Wesley said, "I set myself on fire, and people come to see me burn."

F. I was in Rochester, New York, a few years ago and I was walking downtown. They have a statue of John Wesley. The inscription said, "No man ever came to a town and affected a city like Wesley." I think that is the key. There is such a fire, that it draws people.

And yet, for that to happen there is a price that must be paid. Everyone says they want God to move. But the problem is that the people must be willing to pay the price for revival. It will cost you everything—your "me" time, your mall time, your entertainment time. Everything! A lot of people want to have a move of God while sitting in their La-Z-Boy, with a soda in one hand and the remote in the other. But it doesn't work that way.

And that's why—and you can call them old timers—but back in the forties and fifties, when they had such great moves of God, they were willing to pay the price. I think about my own dad. Here was a team of five or six—or ten or twelve counting the wives—that worked hard jobs, got in their cars after work and drove two to three hours in time to get to the meeting. And they didn't get finished at 8 or 9 o'clock. I remember at times, just getting home with enough time for my dad to get changed and go to work at a cotton mill early in the morning.

This was their lifestyle. And the meetings back then weren't two or three days; they were ten to twelve days at a time. If there is one thing missing today, it is this: *we want God to come down in a weekend and fix instantaneously what has taken us twenty-five years or more for us to get into.*

N. Now they just want it done on a Sunday morning.

R. Weren't you involved in the "Cornfield Revival?" Tell us about that.

F. Yes, Smithton. Steve Gray is the pastor. We met them in 1985 and have been going there for about 25 years. They started in 1984. We had met at a conference and he invited us to come and speak. One of the interesting things about the Smithton revival is that the people would take their vacations when we came—not to go to the Ozarks, but to be in the meetings. They knew the meetings would go long, so they planned for it.

Year after year we would go. And Steve had such an open heart to see God move—he and Kathy both. God gave him a church that wanted the same thing, not just a nucleus within the church. His whole church was the nucleus.

N. He wanted the entire church to run after God. He wanted everyone to tithe, pray and desire the same thing. He wanted them to, in a sense, "walk as one man into Jerusalem."

F. In all the years we would go and simply add more to it. We would start to have great crowds—standing room only. (It was a much smaller building at that time.) But people would come from many other churches. They had been paying the price and God moved. And it just happened in March, 1996. That's when the outpouring began.

N. Before that, they would pray once-a-week for two-and-a-half years specifically for revival.

F. Not about other things. But they prayed—from the gut—laying on the altars for revival. They really cried out.

R. Is the revival still going?

F. Yes, of course it's in Kansas City now. It's strong now. Two years ago they had a fresh blowing of the wind. They've been going every Thursday through Sunday. In November, 2008,

Daystar picked up on it. They've been broadcasting it live every Friday night. People are coming to it from everywhere.

I remember when revival broke out, we were in Mississippi. Steve was calling us every night for advice on what to do. Our hearts were rejoicing with them and encouraging them but I wanted to see that happen in many places. My flesh wanted to go back and join them because there is a certain notoriety with this revival. But our heart is to see this happen in all of the places we go. That's why we're out here. We are here to ignite the fire and make sure it doesn't go out.

7

John Kilpatrick

Apostle of Revival
August 12, 2011

John Kilpatrick experienced firsthand the Glory of God as Holy Spirit entrusted to him the pastoral oversight of the Brownsville Revival in Pensacola, Florida. He now travels extensively across the nation spreading the fires of revival and impacting churches around the world through media ministry.

After nearly forty years of pastoral ministry, twenty-two years of which was his tenure at Brownsville Assembly of God, he and his wife Brenda are fulfilling their apostolic call by establishing churches and mentoring ministers. His hunger and passion for God's presence awakens and stirs the hearts of many to cry out for a move of God.

꧁ ꧂

Pastor John Kilpatrick met Pastor Pete Mullins and me at his office with a big handshake and a big heart. His demeanor was serious almost the whole time we talked and he spoke as a father who had a deep burden for the nation and a passion for revival.

Most interesting to me was Pastor Kilpatrick's emphasis on humility as a prerequisite to revival. (I am reminded of the humility of William Seymour, about whom Frank Bartleman said, "He was a black man, blind in one eye, very plain, spiritual, and *humble*.")

Kilpatrick's insights were very enlightening, especially his statement that one of the keys to sustaining revival is not offending the Holy Spirit.

The Interview

R. Tell us what revival means to you, just in general.

J. I think revival is the only survival for our nation, in a nutshell. It's revival, or else. We've strayed so far in America and in the American Church—though not all, but most of the churches. Once you've made a slight left turn it doesn't take long to be way off track. You begin to accept homosexuality; you begin to accept church without the gifts of the Holy Spirit—without the moving of the Holy Spirit—without the presence of God. And as the Church goes, so goes the world.

So you have a smattering of churches out there trying to hold the line. But they are tagged "right-wing fundamentalists or radicals" and that kind of thing. But when revival takes place—when people are touched by God—they all of a sudden look at you differently. But revival is survival for this nation.

R. What are the necessary ingredients for revival?

J. Well, number one, without a doubt, is prayer. You've got to have prayer. Before revival broke out at Brownsville, I did away with preaching on Sunday nights. When I did, it was a major, major move back in those days for an Assemblies of God church. Sunday nights were your best evangelistic service of the whole week.

I was in the church one day praying, after we had dedicated the new building, and the Lord said, "If you will return to the God of your childhood—if you will make this a house of prayer—I will pour out my Spirit here."

I honestly said to the Lord, "I was raised in prayer so I know what that means, but I also know this means it will be the least attended crowd out of the week. This is a new building and we have to pay the bills." And I said, "Help me!" He said, "I'll give you a plan."

So I started the prayer banners on Sunday night. I had twelve of them. And if you prayed five minutes around each banner, then that makes an hour. I thought my church—because it's a Pentecostal, Assemblies of God, Holy Spirit-filled church—was praying, but I came to realize that if Brownsville was not praying—because of time constraints and weariness and family obligations—if they're not praying, then no one is praying.

I came to realize that the church was not praying. They were "tipping" God every now and then, respecting God, and loving God, but they weren't praying. So when we introduced the prayer banners and we began to pray on Sunday nights—we would have

Holy Communion, which is the Bread of Presence, then we'd have organized prayer, and then we'd have everyone gather in a home room around a banner.

A prayer banner captain would share prayer needs that night and after five minutes of prayer, background instrumental music would begin and everyone would rotate from banner to banner—however they wanted to do it.

At first we were praying an hour, because it's easy to pray five minutes around something that's holding your attention—schools, pastors, warfare, or healing. You can pray easily five minutes when you can look up and see what you are praying about. But then I noticed that the prayer meetings were going about two hours. The people got used to praying and then really got into the groove of what prayer meant.

The banner that always got the most attention was the revival banner. We prayed two-and-a-half years around the prayer banners. Revival broke out two-and-a-half years later on Father's Day. So the first prerequisite to revival is prayer.

The second prerequisite—and I'm not saying that I'm this way, but I'm just giving my observation—the second one is humility. I'm not talking about false humility; I'm talking about true humility. You've got to have it if God is going to send revival. If you don't, then you are going to brag about it—throw your chest out—and you're going to lose it immediately. You've got to be truly humble. God said, "If my people who are called by name shall humble themselves and pray." He said when that happens, "I'll hear and I'll help."

However, I'm troubled by what I see in churches today because I have never seen such a self-centered generation in my lifetime—and I'm talking about really self-centered. They want to be noticed and will do anything to be noticed. A lot of it is a breakdown of home and family, but a lot of it is nothing but pure flesh—the flesh needing attention.

Revival will never come to a man like that. And I'd like to say something else—and I would like for you not to take this wrong, because I don't mean it wrong—but God does not send revival to a city, God does not send revival to a church; He does not send revival to a denomination; *He sends it to a man.*

A church cannot manage revival—there are too many varying opinions. A denomination cannot manage revival. It may be affected by revival, and a city may be affected by a revival. But God doesn't send revival to a city; He sends it to a man or to a woman. This sounds arrogant, but it's not meant that way. "He sought for a man."

Revival is also something that you have to love, and something that you have to buy. The Bible says to "buy the truth and sell it not." You can never have revival on borrowed truth. Revival only comes by bought truth. You have to buy and pay for it yourself. It will cost you.

R. Fire doesn't fall on an empty altar.

J. Yes. A lot of people believe something with second-hand information, but they don't have a first-hand encounter. There are a lot of people out there who are Pentecostal because their mother was filled with the Holy Spirit. And there are a lot of people who are Pentecostal because that's the way they were brought up. And they know a pastor who really affected them. So they are still a part of the Pentecostal church, but they've never been baptized in the Holy Spirit.

I remember in the city where my mother and daddy were raised, Troy, Alabama, that there was a statue in the downtown square. It was a Confederate statute. And we drove by it so much that I thought I understood what that statue was all about. But I had never read the plaque. I had gotten so acclimated—so used to it—that I felt as though I was totally familiar with that statue. Until one day I read that plaque—until that time I didn't know what it was.

That's the same way it is in the things of God—Pentecostal things. There have been some who have been around it all their lives and think they know all about it. But they have never, ever experienced a power encounter with God.

God always said, "I'm the God of Abraham, Isaac, and Jacob." The thing is, Abraham was a well digger and an altar builder. He was the first. Abraham was the one God used after the Fall to get back into human affairs.

Abraham would build an altar and whatever he named it would be what he experienced with God. He'd have an experience with God and dig a well. When he dug down and found water, he would name the well what he found out about God.

When Isaac came along—Isaac means "inheritor"—Isaac didn't have to dig any wells or build altars. He was raised in a good home. His daddy was Abraham and his mother was Sarah. He inherited everything. It was easy for him. So what was a "must" for daddy was now a convenience for Isaac.

By the time Jacob came along, what was a must for granddaddy was ridiculous for Jacob. At the turn of the century speaking in tongues or a power encounter with God was a must. But in many Pentecostal churches across America today you have Isaacs in the Church. Most of the Abrahams are gone—the ones who really had to pay the price. But you've got the Isaacs and the Jacobs sitting there. The Isaacs have had it easy and they think everything is nice. By the time the Jacobs come along and sit in the pew, they think this tongues business is absolutely ridiculous. They think, "We can get along without this. Why don't we become like the other churches?"

P. We're seeing this all across our community.

J. But here's what happened, though. Here's the bill. If you're a rascal, and feel like that, then God is going to send you to a bigger rascal's house. And uncle Laban was a bigger rascal than Jacob was. Laban took Jacob to the cleaners. He was a bigger deceiver than Jacob was.

Nevertheless, God did bless Jacob there, at Laban's house. But by the time he left and actually had to face Esau again, he had his hip knocked out of joint and had a power encounter with God Himself. And guess what he did? He dug a well and built an altar just like his granddaddy did.

Here's where I think we are in America. I think we are at a juncture where America is not a godless nation, but that America is a backslidden nation. Because, if you go back in most people's generations—their granddaddy, their great-granddaddy, their grandmother, their great-grandmother—they were God-fearing people—Christians. Many of them were Pentecostal.

Now, with the things we are facing as a nation, America is about to get her hip knocked out of joint. Then, and then only, will God reduce us and humble us. And we'll go back to doing what our grandfathers did. We'll go back to seeking God. The Bible says that Jesus met the woman at Jacob's well. So we knew he built a well. Isaac had to go back and dig out the wells of his father that had been stopped up.

So when you are talking about revival, it is complex. It's not just a simple thing; it's a very complex matter. There are all kinds of complex tentacles associated with revival.

You remember in the Old Testament, in the time of the Judges, every time a judge died, the people backslid. And God would raise up another deliverer who would call Israel back. They would "knuckle down" and serve God. The judge would die and Israel would backslide again and run away from God.

This nation has really backslidden and run away from God. I believe God is in the process, in the next short period of time, to raise up prophets and apostles—true apostles and true prophets—and there is going to be revival and America is going to be brought back to God.

That's my belief. I can't prove that, but that's my belief. For us to get to where we are, we are lacking prayer and we are lacking humility. (That's a long way around the bush!)

R. What else do you think hinders revival and what sustains it?

J. I think what hinders revival—like when revival broke out at Brownsville—people came from a few states, then all fifty states, then from the nations from the world. People came who didn't have a good testimony. They ran after the fire. They came to Brownsville and saw the revival and they wanted to get that fire and take it back home. But they didn't have a good name where they came from. They weren't consistent or faithful.

They came back home and tried to take what God did at Brownsville and force it on others. As a consequence, we got a lot of blame for that, even though we didn't even know these people. One of the greatest hindrances to revival is a bunch of unproven, unbridled, untamed stallions. They came to Brownsville to partake of holy fire and went home and offered strange fire. That turned pastors off and other people off, because they said, "If they're a part of it, then I don't want to be a part of it."

That's one of the major hindrances to revival. Pastors need to never judge a revival based on someone else's report. They need to be there themselves, to see it, taste it, and experience it. You can never judge something by second-hand reports—especially by people who come and who are not really a good representation of what God did.

The second hindrance is this. Whenever I hit the floor on Father's Day, I had just finished a series of sermons on the glory of God. I preached a nine-part series over ten to twelve weeks. And it was a good sermon series—preached well—based on a lot of exhaustive hours studying God's Word.

When I hit the floor, the first thing out of my mouth was, "Lord, what is this?" The first thing He said to me was, "Happy Father's Day!" The second thing He said was, "Why son, this is what you just got through preaching."

Which led me to understand that you can preach something with great fervor—great passion—exhaust the subject—preach it fully and thoroughly, but until you've tasted and experienced it, you don't know what you are talking about. There are a lot of people that, when revival comes, see it on TV, but there's a big difference between sitting in your den or living room watching it on television and actually being there in the atmosphere and going forward and being touched by it.

It's just like watching a trial on TV. People get all kinds of different interpretations of what's going on in the courtroom. And they jump to conclusions and make all kinds of judgments about what is going on without actually being in the courtroom to see and hear and smell.

So I don't know if it's wise to televise revival. There are, however, people who are touched in their homes because when the Word goes forth, faith always arises. But the only thing I'm trying to say is, people draw conclusions about things like that that are wrong conclusions because they weren't in the atmosphere. And that's a hindrance to revival—a hindrance to it spreading. They see it on TV in that atmosphere and they judge that they know all about it. "Oh, I know all about it." No, you don't. Until you are touched, you don't know what you are talking about.

Before revival broke out in Brownsville, my wife was watching TV one morning and called me in there and Rodney Howard Browne was on in Lakeland. She said, "Come here and look at this!" As soon as I saw it on TV, I felt my lip began to snarl. And I thought, "Oh, my God!" But I heard the Lord say to me, "Don't put your mouth on that." And I never did. Revival came to Brownsville in just a matter of a few weeks. I believe if I would have said, "Oh, how stupid that is—look at that man!" I believe I would have withdrawn myself from revival. I believe it wouldn't have come to my church.

I'll tell you the reason why. When Jesus was going to Calvary, remember the little girl who came up to Peter and said, "Hey, you are one of them!" And Peter said, "No, no, no, you've got it all wrong." She kept on, until finally Peter swore, cursed, and said, "I am not His disciple!"

When Jesus was going to Calvary, Peter, theoretically, removed himself from discipleship by saying, "I don't know the man and I am not his disciple." When Jesus rose from the dead, here's what He said, "Go tell my disciples, *and Peter*. The reason He said that was because Peter was no longer His disciple. He knew he had systematically removed himself *with his mouth* from discipleship. So when Jesus rose from the dead, they are out there fishing, they come to shore and Jesus restores him as a disciple. That's what that's all about—"Do you love me?" Because three times he had denied Him. And on that third time, Jesus looked deep into his soul and said, "Do you *really* love me?" So Christ systematically reinstated him.

When Peter denied the Lord, he denied him beside a coal of fire. And when Jesus built that fire on the beach, it was a coal fire, not a wood fire. He used [the sense of] smell to take him back to when he had denied Christ.

When you smell coals burning, it reminds you of cook outs and the Fourth of July and things like that. When Peter denied Christ, that smell was in his head from warming himself by the fire. When Jesus restored him, he restored him by a fire of coals.

We are complex people, and revival is an awesome thing. But when it breaks out, it deals with complex issues—it unravels them. Revival is not church as usual. Revival is a *ramping up* of church as usual. Revival is an escalation of the presence of God to the point that you never experience normal church.

This leads me to say that once you've experienced revival, you run. Once you've experienced the presence of God, to go back to church as usual—you're marred, you're messed up—because you can never be happy. Once you've had your feet under the table of revival, no other table will do. That's why I make it my life's business to pursue the presence of God. That's why I make it my church's business to pursue the presence of God. Nothing else matters to me. That's all that matters.

P. You're singing our song. That's our heartbeat as well—the presence of God.

R. We are a presence-based church.

P. It's our only place of safety.

J. It's what made early Pentecost. When I say "early Pentecost"—I'm sixty one—and I know to a degree what early Pentecost is all about. And I came from a very Pentecostal church, with a Pentecostal pastor who had integrity—a godly man. My church was really stable and strong; so was he. He was really a statesman.

When you've had that in your life, and you see what the Church has deteriorated to, the frustration is, "Lord, will it ever become like that again?" Or is it going to keep going down left field until it winds up somewhere out there in some crazy stuff—which most churches have. Most churches could have church right on without the presence of God.

P. What we've seen, and what we're concerned about, is that those who profess to be Pentecostal in our community, are less and less Pentecostal. The things that we value and we want to make a stand on and pass on to our children are just seemingly not important.

J. It's not. They are afraid of offending people.

P. That's exactly it. I've seen church in my experience in Coweta county—Assemblies of God, Church of God, and other non-denominational Charismatic churches—they've really travelled down the seeker sensitive model. And there are no more gifts of the Spirit in the service, no more speaking in tongues. It's all because they are afraid—and I meet with these pastors—they almost have a complex about being Pentecostal. They almost say, "We're not like them." It's rampant.

J. Actually, what they are saying is, "I'm not Pentecostal." When Peter said, "This is that," preachers today would say, "No, this is not that." They don't want to be associated with "This is that." But if this is not that, then what is this?

There is a shame there with many pastors with Pentecostal roots. The Bible says they will have "a form of godliness, but deny the power thereof." What that means is that when you deny something, you are denied access or denied entrance. It means you are restricted. So they will have a form of godliness, but restrict the Spirit.

R. The term I use is "corralling" the Spirit.

P. Or controlling Him.

J. But He can't be controlled. When He's grieved, He's gone. As the Spirit falls, He'll also lift. As He lights, He can also fly. My job at Brownsville was to keep things from offending the Holy Spirit. I wouldn't let people or situations offend the Holy Spirit.

R. Is that one of the keys to sustaining revival, then?

J. Oh, absolutely. If I knew someone was in sin, someone in the choir, for instance, and they were in adultery or homosexuality, I'd park them in a heartbeat. My head wouldn't rest on my pillow until they were parked, because I didn't care about them as much as I did the Holy Spirit.

Preachers today care more about the people than they do the Person of the Holy Spirit. You have to care more about the presence of the Holy Spirit than you do people. If I found someone in sin, I'd park them—put them on probation—try to help them, but if they never got back on the worship team, it's no skin off my back.

I don't care how talented they were. I don't care if they play the organ and it sounds like heaven on earth. I'd rather have someone who squeaks by and has holiness than someone full of talent and grieving the Spirit of God. A pastor's main job is *not* funerals and weddings and preaching on Sundays and counseling. *His main job is to be a custodian of the presence of God.*

P. And get out of the way of the Holy Spirit.

J. And get out of the way of the Holy Spirit. Now, you may have to deal with people who get out of line, or get over-zealous, or whatever—they may turn people off or cause confusion. I've done that. But I'd rather have wild fire than no fire. A car that's in motion is easier to guide than one sitting still.

So revival is an absolutely wonderful thing, but it's not what a lot of people think it is. I go places where pastors come out dressed to the hilt; they're wild eyed and have this look of anticipation in their eyes. "Brother Kilpatrick, I can't believe you are here! We're believing God for a revival!" But when you get to looking real close, what they're expecting is not revival at all. Instead, they want crowds and recognition, and fame, and being on Christian TV. You just want to shake them and say, "My God! What's wrong with you! That's not revival. That's not it." If true revival comes, you are going to be on your face. You are going to be in the dirt. You can't believe that God is there.

Revival is a lot of things to a lot of different people. But revival is not a cultural thing. When God brings revival, He never puts it on sale. It will always cost you what it cost previous generations.

P. There's never a fire sale.

J. No, never. It will cost you what it cost others. The Bible says to "buy the truth and sell it not." The reason I'm so passionate about revival is that I've bought it. That doesn't mean I earned it. I'm not talking about that. But I mean that I've paid for revival through misunderstandings, major satanic attack, misrepresentation, and persecution. I've paid for it. And after paying the price, it's more valuable to me than it ever was, because I paid for it.

Nobody ever treasures anything unless they pay for it. If it's given to you, you don't treasure it. You don't. It's not good to over-give to a child. They need to earn it. Don't misunderstand me; I'm not saying you "earn" revival. The Bible says to "buy the truth and sell it not."

It's just like Oral Roberts bought the truth on healing. That's why he could preach it so fervently. You only preach fervently what you've experienced—what you've paid for—what you've bought.

Do you preach healing? Have you experienced healing? So did Kenneth Hagin. Those old boys could preach healing. They wouldn't back up an inch. They paid for it.

I could preach revival and never back up an inch. You could never talk me out of it—till my dying breath—because I paid for it. That's where the Church is today. They are not willing to pay for much.

P. Obviously, it's a fallacy to think that we are an exceptional generation—that we are going to get revival in some way that shortcuts the process.

J. It will never happen. I believe something is going to happen in the near future to humble America. I'll never forget when 911 happened. I was watching CNN. Do you remember Judy Woodruff? She was the anchor person. She said that day, or a few days later—a liberal, left-wing reporter—said, "My, it's so hard to believe this has happened. This just leads us to know that we need to return to God."

Then you saw Democrats and Republicans standing on the Capital steps saying, "God bless America." They're not standing on the Capital steps saying "God bless America" now. That only lasted a week or ten days. But something is going to happen in this country that, whenever it hits, people are going to be humbled and they are going to stay humbled for quite some time.

That's when revival is going to come. Revival comes in the worst of times, not the best of times. Do you remember Azusa Street and the Great San Francisco earthquake? It comes in the worst of times. Moody and the Chicago fires? So God is going to touch America, I believe, but it's not going to be like America thinks.

P. We really believe in the presence, and we are a presence-based church, but can you give us some thoughts about a local church positioning itself for revival. If you were to say to a church, this is the position you should be in, what would that be? What is the best way to be in position for the coming revival? What should we pursue?

J. One of the things that was shocking to me about revival was—I was in the church at Brownsville one Saturday night by myself with the lights out—about a year or so before revival broke out.

The Holy Spirit said, "May I bring a sword into this church?" My thought was, "Yes, Lord, absolutely!" Because I thought He was going to cut all my hell-raisers out. And I was shocked. When He brought a sword in the church—when revival came—He cut some of my good people out who were religious. And some of my hell-raisers He used mightily!

It was a shock to me. One of the things I learned about revival is that some of the things you think are a foregone conclusion are tentative. And the ones who are tentative are the very ones God is going to touch and use powerfully, and integrate them in because they are going to be so radically used by God.

Many times the ones who are most solid are the most religious. They are the ones who will tell God how to move and how much they are going to let God move. And we're not used to this, and this is our church, and we're not sure we're going to let you do this here.

Whereas, some of your wild-eyed boys are saying, "Hey God, do what you want to do." They are the ones He'll use. Peter was like this. That's why Jesus gravitated toward Peter. He was impetuous. He wasn't religious; he was impetuous. He's the one God used. He's the one who walked on the water. And the Lord commended him. Everybody else stayed in that boat.

So I think one of the main things a church can do to get in position for revival is: what you talk about will come. If you talk trouble, trouble will come. If you talk lack, lack will come.

P. Heaven is listening to our conversation and God is ready to affirm.

J. Not so much that—it's just a law. It's like gravity. If I climb up on top of this building and jump, there's going to be an accident. There's going to be some blood.

P. *Is it accurate to say, "Watch our preconceived notions"?*

J. Watch preconceived notions, but don't put too much trust in people. Because the very ones you are thinking will be dependable, will wind up being the ones who are religious.

R. Can I ask you one other question? You had mentioned earlier about apostles and prophets. How important are the five-fold ministries to bringing and sustaining revival? We are a part of a ministry that believes in the five-fold ministry mentioned in Ephesians.

J. Before revival broke out, I couldn't even spell "apostle." I mean, I always believed in the five-fold, but I really didn't know what an apostle was. I knew what a prophet was, but not an apostle. I had no background in it; never preached on it. So that didn't have anything to do with bringing revival. But when revival came, it rightly related me to the five fold.

R. How did that happen?

J. Because when revival came—revival is a myth buster. It's a cultural realignment—a Scriptural realignment. It's a measuring stick—you know pretty well where you stand. It's also a revealer of what you have and what you don't have—what's working and what's not working. Revival does those things.

R. It shakes everything.

J. It shakes everything. It's a major realignment. And that's when I began to really realize that the apostolic and revival go together—and the prophetic. And I'm no pushover when it comes to the prophetic. I believe in the prophetic, but I don't believe everyone who says he or she is a prophet is really a prophet. If you are of the truth, people of the truth will find their way to you. And you will find your way to them.

If a person is not of the truth or is a self-appointed or so-called prophet or apostle, that bonding—that clay and iron—will never adhere. I wouldn't say that revival came because of my understanding of the prophetic and apostolic, but when it came, it made me have an understanding of it. That's why I'm real lenient with preachers that fight the prophetic and apostolic because they are not in revival and they don't understand it. It's an ignorance thing, not a willful fighting. It's totally ignorance.

P. As the revival progressed, the fivefold...

J. ...just automatically fell into place.

R. I know you had Steve Hill there, and I would say he's an evangelist.

J. Yes, he's an evangelist.

R. And that would be one of the gifts.

J. Yes, absolutely. When revival comes it's an escalation of the presence of God even in your own personal life. Your candle only burns a certain number of degrees, but during revival it becomes a torch. The spirit of a man is the candle of the Lord, but when revival comes, it's the torch of the Lord. You just see things differently—with greater illumination. You don't struggle to read about them, you just understand them.

That's another problem. Preachers are struggling to understand things, but they are not having revelation. When you are struggling to understand things, you are reading everything you can get your hands on—some of it's good and some of it's bad—but when revelation comes, it's a God-given impartation.

R. Well, this has been really rich. Would you pray for us?

8

Steve Gray

Pastor of World Revival Church
October 29, 2011

Steve Gray, founder and senior pastor of World Revival Church, is a leading voice in global revival. His ministry, with his wife Kathy as co-pastor, impacts literally thousands of churches around the world.

World Revival Church is known worldwide for the reviving presence of God. Since 1996 (the "Smithton Outpouring") and again in 2008 with an upsurge of God's power, what God is doing at World Revival Church attracts the attention of media and visitors from across the globe.

Steve is known for his powerful and scholarly preaching of the Word of God. He has authored several books, including *My Absurd Religion*, an Amazon bestseller, *Hope Heals,* and *When the Kingdom Comes*, a revival classic. He is the writer and producer of the feature film, *Three Blind Saints* and is currently working on a second film as an outreach to Israel, *Something to Believe*.

Together, Steve and Kathy have founded various ministries, with a heart to see everyone experience the powerful presence of God in revival.

ꟸ ꟸ

The people of World Revival Church received me with a genuine warmth and hospitality that is rarely found in churches today. And Pastor Steve Gray kicked his feet up on the chair next to him while he swallowed a piece of chocolate and talked about revival. We were like two long-time friends sitting on a porch in Georgia glad to reflect on the day.

Steve is one of those rare pastors who incorporates revival into his church's culture. And his insights into the "height and depth" of revival clearly demonstrate his seasoned ability to pastor revival.

Steve made several important points about sustaining revival, especially pertaining to these ups and downs. To pastor a revival, the leaders must recognize—either intuitively, or by the Spirit—when the congregation needs to be built up or broken down. Sometimes Christians begin to take God for granted, and they need to be reminded in no uncertain terms who they are *without* Christ's grace. And sometimes Christians get so beaten down that they need a solid dose of encouragement.

I am reminded of the ministry of Jonathan Edwards, who most people know for his sermon, "Sinners in the Hands of an Angry God." But we should not assume that this was characteristic of all his messages. He also recognized the importance of religious affections, including love, desire, hope, joy, and gratitude. I think Edwards knew how to balance the two extremes and that true revivalists must understand the "rhythms" of the congregation in order to sustain revival. Pastor Gray is one who understands these rhythms.

The Interview

R. – What does revival mean to you and what are your thoughts in general about revival?

S. Well, the word "revival" elicits so many different responses that it's a difficult word to use because people label it. Probably the most difficult part for revival in definition has been the traditional idea that a revival is an evangelistic campaign. I had some of that in my mind at first, too, because that's more of the traditional thought of it.

After I was really touched by the power of God in 1996, I spent a few weeks reaching out to what I would call the traditional "lost" or "unsaved," thinking that they were going to come. All of a sudden, as crowds began to increase, I looked to see who these people were. And, yes, you could give an altar call at the end and they would come down. But they were not first-time conversions.

That's the thing that sometimes fools us in revival because the visitor to it would think, "Wow! All these people got saved tonight?" But that was not the condition I was finding. I was finding that most of these were people who were long-term believers, but they came in pretty bad shape.

I realized they needed something. And that's when I began to understand revival—what it is. We've got millions of people who have confessed the right thing, they've gone to church, they've participated and yet they've been turned into something half dead.

That's what I see revival is: bringing life to the half-dead—bringing them back to life again. Revival doesn't mean you bring someone back to life again as though they were dead and brought back to life. In revival they are not dead; they are just half dead. I started realizing, "Wow! Look at the shape of these people!" And I think it's gotten worse.

In '96, '97, and '98, there was a real hunger for God—a hunger that sparked revivals. But now the people are even more beaten down, almost where they are reluctant to even try again. Most of the lack of hunger and desire has been, in my opinion, the result of what traditional religion has done to church people.

I realized there weren't many people ministering to the people in the pews. Nobody was pastoring these people who had already not been pastored properly for years. Instead of pastoring, ministers had been put through the system of creating successful ministries. That's not necessarily all bad, but we've been creating successful ministries for about twenty-five years, probably, and not creating successful Christians—at the expense of Christians. Therefore, churches look good, but it's a lot of whitewash, because nobody's really dealing with what is going on behind the scenes in these ministries.

So the biggest problem I've had is people expecting evangelistic campaigns and then they don't want to admit that we—the Christians—are the problem. I spent a lot of time studying the Scriptures and came away with the idea that Jesus had the same opinion.

When he started His ministry, He went right to the people of God. He wouldn't get off of them because He realized that that was the problem. If they could get it right, then they could become the light of the world. If we can get it right, then we could have more of a Great Awakening than a revival.

When I started saying that to people, it started opening some eyes. Just think about Jesus; He never once ministered to the Romans—He never once attacked them, He never pointed His finger, He didn't slam His fist down on the pulpit and say, "There's your problem."

On the other hand, the Pharisees did point the finger. The religious people of Jesus' day were saying that Rome was our problem and praying, "God come down and deliver us from Rome."

Jesus was saying, "No, Rome's here because you were the problem. If you weren't the problem, Rome would never have gotten here in the first place.

So I see such a parallel with that in revival. I began to realize that there is hardly anyone out there ministering to those people—pastoring, reviving the millions of people who have been through the religious system—people who either don't go to church anymore or who are just sitting there surviving. These are people who aren't sure what to believe and are reluctant to hope that it's going to be as big as they expected. It's like the old song titled, "Is that All There Is?" They have this feeling, "Is this it?"

Then you come up against the battle with those who are running the religious system—defending their position, which is what the Pharisees did. So you have this tremendous problem: the uninformed who think maybe revival is supposed to be about getting everybody saved.

However, think of it in these terms: if you have a bad marriage, you don't solve it by having more kids. And that's what we have in our churches. We have a bad "marriage" on our hands and all we're trying to do is get more "kids." And the "family's" just becoming more dysfunctional. That was my take on it, anyway.

So I thought, I need to try to help these people and stop this dysfunction in the church. I had to emphasize that revival is not an evangelistic campaign where we just need to get more people saved.

I had to get a message that would not allow the people to get away with their dysfunction. And, at the same time, help them realize that in some ways it's not their fault. So in all my messages I hit some things pretty tough, but I try to be myself and make it as fun as I can, while at the same time being serious about it until the very end, where I try to leave them hope.

There is hope. It's hard, but it's not that hard. If you're willing to look at the problem, stop blaming everybody else, and set a new priority, then God's always said, "Return to me and I'll return to you. Draw near to me and I'll draw near to you."

I will add that the obstacles in that journey are pretty hard because you've got people going to a church that's still building a ministry and not building the people up. You've got those in ministry positions who are deceiving the people by appearing like they really, really care about them.

I've often put a question mark on some of the phrases we use today, like "seeker sensitive." And, of course, we need to be seeker sensitive. But what really happened? Did a pastor wake up one day with a revelation that says, "You know what, I need to be more sensitive to people"? Or did he go to a conference where he saw that a church was exploding in growth and money and power in the community, and ask, "Aha, how did you do that?"

"Well, we started drinking coffee in the service and wearing shorts and sandals and shortening the service, and telling people how special they are." So they started a technique because that's what they wanted—a successful ministry in the guise of being more sensitive. So what happened is that the people just got worse, because it is a little deceptive.

So revival to me is exactly what it's always been—it's God coming down to bring back to life those that have become half-dead in the pews and set everything aright for His own people. And it would be easy if we didn't have so many people defending their positions.

Your hope is that things don't have to get a whole lot worse before they get a whole lot better. We can make it better now. But I find that right now with the world and economy and with governments changing and toppling, there's a little more sense of anxiety in the air—and instability—which I think is going to actually help the cause of revival.

The ministers and pastors and leaders and evangelists who can help people in their dysfunction (as opposed to what Jesus didn't do, such as ranting and raving about how the homosexual community bringing judgment on America) can help the cause of revival. Those that rant about judgment coming because of the homosexuals are like Jesus saying that the Roman bath orgies are going to bring judgment on Israel. No they're not. They have no power over us. We're going to bring judgment on ourselves because we have lost our heart for God.

If I was going to say how we are going to save America, I'd say all we need to do is get the Church on track—where it needs to be—where the people of God are who they say they are. We need to set a priority and stop telling the people that we can take all these things and put Jesus on our list and church on our list and soccer on our list—we need to get back to a priority.

If you can get people to seek first the kingdom of God, and love Him first and make some real priority calls that may seem sacrificial in some ways, we can have revival. What seems sacrificial is not, because you can really turn your family when you set Jesus as a priority—you don't have to lose your kids nor have rebellious teenagers.

Getting the mindset that Jesus needs to have a better position in our lives will bring revival. It's easy to do if we can get a priority change. But it's hard to get people to understand that that's where the problem lies. So that's what I do and that's what revival is to me. It's getting the people of God to come back to God. And there He is.

R. And by that I don't think you mean that as disciples, these people aren't going to reach the world—that as disciples, they're required to reach the world, too—but as a byproduct.

S. Yes, the end of the road is that we are going to reach the world and have the outreach we want. I suppose, too, though, that we have to ask ourselves that as we are building ministries and doing all this, how really interested are we in saving the world? Or are we really interested in just getting better attendance and calling it outreach?

R. Yes, just getting more funds for the program.

S. I can't make that judgment call on everybody. That's not my place. That's the Lord's place to make that call. But it's a worthwhile question.

We hear people say we need to get more people saved, but sometimes it feels more like a church growth program, rather than, "Do we really care about those people"? Because, if we really care about the people, then I don't think we would be preaching and teaching the things that we do.

In fact, I tell people that my experience has been that most people have not heard the gospel. What we call the gospel and what really *is* the gospel are two different things.

First of all, the first verse in Mark says, "The gospel about Jesus Christ." And the second is that Jesus went about preaching the gospel of the kingdom of God. What we have now is more a combination of humanism, Sigmund Freud, and Jesus Christ. Everyone wants to be self-analyzed. So they aren't really getting the power of the gospel. It's like alcoholics anonymous—give me three steps. We've gone through that for so long.

When I found my life in trouble—I had been in the ministry for a long time, and I found my life going downhill fast. The bottom line was that most of it was my fault. But the second line of it was that the Church system doesn't know how to handle anybody who is struggling with anything anyway—even though you can't tell people that. The other thing is that there is such a mean-spirited, judgmental, tabloid society now that everybody is eager to expose everybody.

So, as a pastor or leader, once they decide they don't like you anymore, they have to justify why they don't like you, so they are going to find something wrong with you, rather than just leave your church and go to another church and say, "They're fine; I just needed something fresh." Maybe it's deeper than that, but let's do it respectfully.

Instead, they have to take people with them and say something bad and justify the move. Every pastor you talk to has been through that—people finding fault with you, finding reasons to leave. Plus, we know that leadership isn't perfect anyway.

And we live in a very rebellious, self-centered society, where people often say, "You're not meeting my needs, so I'm going to 'divorce' you—leave the church. All of this mind frame is going on, so when they leave a church, it's just like a divorce. The guy she said she loved is now the biggest rat in the world. And she tells everybody that.

That happens to pastors and leaders. After years and years of that, you don't know who you are anymore. You think, "Maybe I *am* a bad guy." You start looking at your own life and maybe you haven't been the best husband or the best dad. And it starts wearing on you.

With me, as it got worse, I found out that some of the people we got the closest to, turned out to be the ones who turned on us the most. That's why they always advise you as a pastor not to get close to the people—and that's like, how do you do that and still pastor them?

R. Do you find these things hindering revival?

S. Well, actually, I find these symptoms more *bringing* leaders to revival—if they realize that it's the system we are in that's causing them to have these symptoms. Although, that's not total. Some of it was my fault. But when it came down to it in my crisis, I gave God every opportunity to do whatever He wanted to do with me—somewhere between retire me and kill me. But I never gave Him the option to do what He did to Paul on the road to Damascus. I prayed, "Why can't you just break the heavens and flash your light and knock me down and change me?" Well, I never gave Him that option, because I didn't even know it existed.

I think that the leadership and the people are so worn down now, that a true revival is really the answer for them—a true move of God. But I think most are like me—so blinded and so beaten down—so afraid to try again—that they don't try that option. However, I'm thankful that I have realized that there are thousands to millions of people out there—in pretty bad shape—that are starting to think that maybe there's no other answer but a move of God. And that's good.

R. So the failure of the Church is actually leading it to revival—that there is no other option.

S. In my estimation. I tell people that the alternative to revival is the unthinkable.

Traditionally, what religious people have done over a long period of time, (and what the Jews did—if they didn't choose revival)—was to mix themselves with other philosophies, ideas, and religions. If we don't choose revival—and this is my spiritual guess, if there is such a thing as that—other religions, particularly Islam, will continue their march and not change their course for anything.

Islam will continue its march forward, and we'll be such beaten down people—lukewarm, beaten down, with no backbone—that we won't fight it and we'll just become a mixture of Judaism and Babylon and Molech worship and idolatry. It'll be a deception to us since they'll not mix with us, but we'll mix with them—because we are so weak.

R. In a way, you could say that—just looking at the population of Islam in the Detroit area—you could look at that as a bridgehead for Islam, or an opportunity for revival.

S. Yes, and the problem is that revival in the Muslim communities is not up to the Muslims. It's up to us. We're the carriers, not them. They don't decide our fate; we decide our fate.

That's difficult though, because we're not in very good shape. We're having a hard time just getting people out of bed on Sunday morning to go to church. And we think we're going to change a whole nation of people who follow Allah, where many are willing to die for what they believe? That's a pretty tall order, but not impossible. It's been done before.

So it's basically in the hands of the people of God, not in anyone else—not in the homosexual community or the movie producers—our fate is in our hands and our relationships. And we can be unstoppable if we get it right.

So, boy, getting people to turn to the Lord—you wouldn't think it would be so hard, but there are so many options today, so much entertainment, so many distractions—and they are addicted to it. In a kind of clever way, they don't realize they are addicted to it. But when you try to have a move of God, the first battle you face is, "Ah, am I going to have to go to church more?"

So, rather than people who want to give more, they're like, "I'd love to have something happen in our church, but I heard you guys go to church—how many days a week? Does it mean I've got to go to church more?"

It happens to the pastors, too. And they don't just wonder if they want to do it, they are not even sure they *could* do it.

But, of course, that's without the power of God. You're looking at your life on your own, wondering if you could do this. But if you did step into it, you'd realize that you could do it—and what a great life it is. It just changes you. Revival—the Bible—becoming a new creation—a new race of people—transformed. Right now we're kind of stuck because we haven't experienced anything like this before.

I have seen so many changed. It just takes a twinkling of an eye. Bang! It's done. But getting people there to where their guard is down—their hope is up—their suspicions are set aside so that God can work in their lives—all these things are the battle.

I went through a battle. It was short-lived. You go through the "manifestation" battle where you go to a revival and maybe see some things you hadn't seen before. You wonder if it was the devil or if it was God. And you have to get over that.

The way I got over it was that I got so desperate for God that I said, "I don't care—I'm not the devil and the devil's not going to do it to me—I'm so desperate—I need God—I just don't care anymore. I'm just not going to fight that battle."

It was a battle that was keeping me far from God. I just finally had to trust. I got over that, so I realized how hard I needed to run, at least for a season—to pursue and set a priority. I had to come to the point where nothing mattered anymore.

Actually, I felt like I was about to lose everything anyway. I could have lost my ministry, my family, marriage—everything. I had to realize, no matter what happens, I've got to get my life back and I've got to meet Jesus for real. If my church doesn't want me anymore, so be it. If my wife doesn't want me anymore, so be it. I'm going to find out what this is.

So I pounded the floor and cried out and did things I hadn't done before in pursuing God. I was so desperate. Then, bang! I got there. You seek; you find. But I didn't understand the level of seeking. I think I had my own definition of seeking. It was pretty weak. I didn't know what seeking is to God. But I learned. So I encourage people with that.

One of the things I do that encourages people a lot in revival—and my wife thinks it's a gift—is my ability to create a hunger in people. If I can get them hungry, they do the rest of the work themselves.

So I go into a church—and I can usually change a church in twenty-four hours, especially if I can get two services in twenty-four hours—or Saturday night, Sunday morning, and Sunday night. If I can get three services, I can really turn things around.

If you give me an average, good church where the people sincerely desire to move on in God—whatever level they want to—I can go into there and by the end of the second service you won't even recognize them anymore.

Usually, it's because I tap into a latent hunger. There's a hunger for God that I search for in them. If I can tap into their hunger, they start doing the work themselves. They're glued to the sermon, because their hunger is gluing them to it. They listen and by the time I say, "Would you like me to pray for you?" the intensity is so heavy. But it's based on their hunger, not my preaching, really.

R. How do you get the leadership of that church to sustain that kind of revival?

S. That's a tough one. That's been *the* tough one. We are one of the few, if any, that have been able to sustain revival. I can tell you the story of 1996, and you can still see it today just as hot as ever. Tonight. Tomorrow. And every week.

During all those years, the American people have been up and down—they haven't always been as hungry for revival. When they were super hungry, crowds would come up, people would come, a story would be written on us and then you would go through a season where they would run after it, then cool off.

So people assume that because it's not in the press, or that visitors aren't lining up to get in, that it's still not happening. But it never really let up here. And in 2008 we had a new upsurge at World Revival Church that was less dramatic but has carried us the last few years.

So I think that, since you spoke with John Kilpatrick—if I can use him—he and I have some different styles and different ways of doing things, but when I went to Brownsville, I stayed for the Sunday service. A lot of the visitors went to Steve Hill's services and then left—probably going back to their own churches, but I stayed for the Sunday service. John Kilpatrick did the Sunday service and Lindell Cooley, I think, did the music. John also did communion and preached the sermon. Afterwards, I called back home—this was at the lowest point in my life—and said, "Kathy, I've just been in the best Sunday morning service I've ever been in my life." And the reason is, I said, "I think this guy pastors this revival even though he's not the front man." That planted the thought, "Aha! A move of God can be pastored." I realized that a move of God can be, and needs to be, pastored.

So I came home, after being touched by the power of God, and kept the fire and utilized renewed pastoring skills. And that is why we have been able to sustain it.

Unfortunately, so many people who were touched by the fire of God didn't plan on it—they've been feeding their congregations candy, waiting for this fire to fall. But when the fire falls, they've had them on such a diet of candy that they can't switch them over to meat that fast. And the people get confused.

If you tell people to come down and just say this prayer and just do this, and they just do that, and then you go and get all on fire for God and come back and say, "Now we're going to have revival and have three services or four services a week." The people go, "This isn't why I came to this church. You told me to say the prayer and show up when I want to."

So the difference was that I went on a two-and-a-half year revival search before it happened in my life. All the while I was praying for revival with my congregation and planting seeds. When it snapped, I had some groundwork done. Then I had to pastor it and not be afraid to move the pieces around in the revival. Most pastors I saw, when God began to move, were afraid to touch it. They thought, "The Holy Spirit will stop if I touch it." But I wasn't afraid of that.

For instance, God would move in our services during worship and people would get healed. I could have sent everyone home, but I said, "No, we're going to have everyone sit down, and now we're going to hear some preaching." I realized that some people are reached through the worship and some people are reached through the breath of God, but with other people, only the Word of God convinces them. That's their make-up. So I almost always—with a very few exceptions—have preaching in every service.

When we were in Smithton, I preached and preached and preached and preached. And that's what sustained us. Unfortunately, many who got touched by revival put the Word of God at a low priority—almost like it was old fashioned. I know, I got criticized for making it a priority.

When we moved to the city, I started wearing a suit. I was dressing down when I was out in the country. I was dressed then like ministers dress now. I decided that I could reach more people if I started dressing up more. Because those people who used to go to church handled the suit and tie better than they did the "dress down" look. So I did it for them. Then I got criticized for dressing up because others said, "He dresses up. He preaches old-fashioned messages. And we come and just float in the presence of God."

Well, those places aren't floating now. They've gone through it, remade their mistakes, and have another generation where there's nothing of revival anymore. They've got to start all over again.

With us, we have people who were touched in the revival in '96 who are still here—the kids who were there—little kids who were there in '96 who are grown up, married, and I have their little kids here now.

R. And they're expecting church to be this.

S. Yup. And that's all they've ever known. And now I've got the parents that were there who are now grandparents standing with their grandchildren with their hands in the air worshipping God. And I'm one of them. I've got my grandchildren here. My daughter, my son-in-law J. D. King who runs the network, and my grandkids are in the midst of this and there is nothing like that in the whole world—three generations worshipping on the same page.

There are no questions about who we're going to be or who we're going to serve. There's just no battle. I'm having the time of my life with my family, and my brothers and sisters and their kids—all their grandkids are here. So whatever happened there in the early days of revival, we were able to sustain it. I think pastoring it with the Word of God did it.

R. What do you say to pastors who are afraid of revival, or afraid of the cost of revival—the long hours or the crowds of people who come, or the mechanics behind the scenes to shepherd all of that? Tell me a little more about pastoring the revival.

S. I decided that I couldn't do it all. Like Moses was told, "You're not going to be able to do it all." So Kathy and I were praying for everybody every service, and preaching and I thought, "You know, I can do this for so long, and only so long."

One lady stood up in a service and said, "We're going to be doing this until Jesus returns." It was just a wild statement, but I thought, "I don't know if I can be praying for all these people until Jesus returns."

So the first thing I did was start raising up prayer warriors to be used spontaneously, in reserve. I trained them and I prayed for them.

Then, as the weeks went by, any time I felt a sense of fatigue, I would use them. I'd pray for people, then I'd stop, call for the prayer warriors—however many—ten to twenty maybe—pray for them, and then I'd turn them loose and I'd go sit down.

The amazing thing is, when it was done right, we didn't lose any of the anointing. There were a few people whose faith level was a little higher when I prayed for them, and they'd follow me around like you've seen in other revivals, but after awhile, people realized that this was the Holy Spirit; this isn't the work of a man.

So I still use that today. I still have prayer warriors lined up every service. I can go out to pray, but if I'm feeling fatigued or my voice is getting tired, we can have our prayer warriors come. They can go out, and they know how, and they can sweep through the place with the anointing, and people are not disappointed after the experience because God shows up.

That was one way I pastored the revival. Another way was to get really organized so that everybody knew their job. Back then I had to have a lot of volunteers, because I didn't have any other staff. So raising up dedicated volunteers is important—and help them understand that this is their revival.

I've noticed what happens in bigger churches when they experience revival is that they have visitors come and their own people stop coming. With ours, however, I gave the revival to them. I said, "This is yours." I made them car parkers, ushers, prayer warriors, helpers on the front lines—just anything we could do to host the revival. And they felt that they had to be there.

So the Smithton congregation showed up for every service—with their kids. We had six services a week; that's a lot. But they looked at me and expected me to be there, so they were there, too. Of course, they had to work all day and then show up. It was quite a challenge. But that's how it was pastored—delegating it out and not being afraid that…

R. It can't be a one-man show.

S. Correct. And that was the beauty of it and part of the sustaining power for the revival. Of course, as a leader, I can't be afraid to give some of it up. I don't want to be a one-man show. I have to enjoy—I have to be a father, a pastor who enjoys watching other people succeed. They're my folks. I trained them. It's no insult to me to see them do well. It's a compliment to me if they can do it without me.

So that's really, really where I've been in revival to where it's so powerful now. We've got people, young ones—in their '40s, and '30s, and '20s—different levels—that are so well-trained in this that I could not do anything in the service and it would just flow without me. And they are good preachers—really good, good preachers and presenters and worshippers.

The other thing, though, I did to help sustain revival—and I think is a lacking in most revivals—is when they say that God shows up. It's really a revelation—everyone gets a new revelation of who God is. And, hopefully, we'll have some signs and wonders and miracles and healings. That's pretty exciting.

But if you stay immature in that place, then you want to keep duplicating that and duplicating that. I saw that with a lot in the churches in the '90s. After awhile they were just showing up and trying to make something happen. And it was just dying.

Now, what I did, as a pastor wanting the move of God to continue, was to somehow be able to balance what I call the height of revival and the depth of revival. Because, for me personally, the first few minutes were high—deepening things—but, as I walked in revival, God began to deal with who I was.

He didn't just show up and say, "I'm great, and you're great." He'd show up great and the more I'd stand with Him, the more I realized, "I'm not so great." I began to shrink. I began to be dwarfed. I was getting smaller, as it should be.

And as I did that, I'd go to the depths, and sometimes I'd show up in the service and God would reveal Himself to me—and it was such a high. And the next service I might show up and He might reveal me to me. He wasn't revealing Himself, but me to me. You know what, that wasn't a "height." I went down. "Woe is me! I am undone!"

Once I realized that, I thought, "If I can catch that"—the balance of the height and depth of revival, we can sustain it. It's a matter of knowing when to walk on the heights with the people and knowing when they've had enough of the heights and it's time to have a revelation of who we are in the presence of Him. Then you go down.

Now, all of a sudden your sermons and your moments—Oh! The depths! People are crying and you see them rushing down and falling on their face, and all that. But if you keep that up too long, they start feeling too low, too bad. Their eyes get on themselves. And now you've got to get them back to the revelation of who God is.

I came up with a formula that "height plus depth equals length." And I got length by knowing when to play the height and the depth—when to do it.

Now, some services you might have both. But, what I found out is that some revival services went all to the height because they had been so down. And others, though, because of their upbringing, had been in the more legalistic way, so that when revival came, they started beating everyone with holiness. "You're not worthy to have a revival." And people just wore themselves out. They wore out from the height because they almost made it entertainment, and they wore out in the depth because they got so beaten so badly.

So what I do all these years—either I just have a gifting or just wisdom to know when to play what—is balance out the height and depth. When I feel like they could turn this into a frivolous thing, where they start taking for granted the height of signs and wonders and healings—I take them to the depth and they are all of a sudden crying out for God.

R. Remember where we came from.

S. Yes, remember where we came from. And then combine it, or move it or something so it's a balance between that. And that keeps a congregation going in revival.

R. Is there a kind of a rhythm to this, or is this totally a sense of the leading of the Spirit?

S. Well, I've never been asked a question like that before. I like your insight on that. There really is a rhythm to revival. But I've never had anybody ever ask me that question. The simple answer is that you just let God talk to you.

But there's a rhythm to it. Most of the time, I know the rhythm before I show up. How I'm going to do it might be more spontaneous. I have had a lot of experiences where I would get a little flash of a picture in my mind, and then I just need to act out the picture.

For instance, when I'm worshipping God and a little flash comes—perhaps a picture of all of our teenagers lined up. I just wait for the moment when we ought to do it, and "Bang!" God shows up as we follow through on the "picture." But it's not a form; it's just what I saw, so that's what I did. And it works. The rhythm of it is very important—the rhythm of the worship, too.

There was only one other person that I was able to have this conversation with. That was Ruth Heflin. Kathy was able to minister with her in her very last crusade she had before she passed away. Kathy was there with her Ruth and I had a wonderful discussion with how even the tempo of a song affects the anointing in a revival.

You can sing a song a hundred times, but this time it needs to go slower—but this time it needs to go faster. This applies to musicians and pastors, but I find pastors that don't know music often withdraw—they just let some guy handle the worship and then they get up as the big guy swinging the bat to bring revival. But for me, I don't do that. I don't look like I'm pastoring during worship, but I am. If the song's too fast or too slow, even if we've done it a hundred times, I'll send a signal to slow it down. If they don't see my signal, then eventually I'll walk up to them. So I'm pastoring even the music, but not micro-managing every second.

R. Yes, not domineering over everything.

S. No, because I want them to learn to do this. My joy would be to do nothing—just worship with everybody else. But I'm down on the floor with the people, not up on the platform—down with the people, feeling the rhythm of it. You're exactly right.

And when I come into a service, whether it's mine or whether it's at a church I'm visiting where I've never been before, I always try to ask them—because they try to put me up front or on the platform—so I ask to be down with the people, but a little to the side, because I need to look over my shoulder and see where the rhythm is happening with the people. It helps me know what to do next. So that's a good observation.

R. It's always a sensitivity to the Spirit's leading.

S. And probably skill without fear. You have to not have fear and not be frivolous either. So there are little things we learn to help protect revival. You wouldn't think that being organized is a part of helping maintain revival because most people think that organization takes away from the Spirit, but without it, the revival becomes just free-for-all.

We found that if we got really organized and everyone knew what they were supposed to do, then we found that a lot of the weird spirits that come in to mess up revival either didn't come, or, if they did, they were shut down. We just didn't have that much of a problem with this like other places did. And after analyzing it, I think they came in to our services and felt the decency and the order of the place and thought, "There's no opening for me here." There was such freedom and such results, but there wasn't any opening for weird spirits to do whatever they wanted.

We never had that many experiences, but we had a few times when somebody would break through. We had the "Prophet Jeremiah" say he was here. He had a big scroll on his shoulder. He seized a moment when a lady was healed at the back—instantly healed of something and she screamed, "I'm all healed!" When everybody turned around to see, including the ushers, "Jeremiah" came forward and laid out his scroll on the floor. But that was a rare occasion. We didn't have that many weird manifestations.

I felt like our services were biblical and orderly and our people just learned. And we continued to die to ourselves and not want to display ourselves and things just worked well. So organization was really important and it is very organized here. Again, everybody's doing their job and they trust their pastor, they trust me enough that I can just let the freedom go because I don't have to make sure that everyone's in their place and the music is going to be good.

But when I first started, I'd walk in and if the air conditioner is not right, or the heat's not right, I'd immediately notice and say, "We've got to have as many things right as possible because we don't want any distractions." You have to be a multi-level person to pastor revival.

With so many people pastoring these days where the system is set up that doesn't work well. (I wouldn't have said this years ago, because it might have sounded arrogant, but with the mileage

I have on me now I can.) I just think that most men and women out there are not made to be a senior pastor leading a movement all by themselves. Most of them should be team players.

It may never happen, but if we really wanted to have a great move of God, then a community—not a denomination, but a community—should get together and decide who is the most anointed one to be the speaker. Who's the most anointed one to be the evangelist; who's the most anointed one to be counseling these people? Because some people are really great at counseling and some are really terrible at being preachers. Then, instead of having all these churches everywhere with twenty, thirty, forty of fifty people, we could come together and really have a community of churches where we would find great success.

Instead, we've got all these little churches out here trying to be everything. And, I had people here who did that too, and then they joined me and I told them, "This is my calling on my life. If you'll help me, then I can be what I need to be. But I can't be in here counseling every day, listening to their problems every day, and fulfill what I'm supposed to do. Would you be willing to do this?"

Well, I happened to find guys who were so beat up by the system and who had been the one-man show. They said, "Man I'd love to be on a team!" It's really been beautiful here. And I've learned my lesson from that. A lot of people should be on a team.

When you're trying to translate this out to a local pastor who wants to have a move of God in his church, is he—or she—really able to be the carrier all by himself? You've got to have some good callings on your life.

R. Let me ask you a question that's somewhat related to what you are talking about. What do you think about the five-fold ministry that's expressed in Ephesians 4:11 and has that had an impact on your revival or is that something you desire to incorporate into revival—all the ministries, apostle, prophet, evangelist, pastor and teacher—in what you are doing, or have you already done that?

S. I would like to see it more. I have it laid down, but the people who want to be a prophet are the strangers who wander in and tell me they are a prophet, or an apostle. And I can't be a good father or pastor to these people who wander in and out, and then they get offended. Maybe they're real apostles, but most of them are walking around looking for someone to say they are, because the local church they came out of said, "I don't think you are."

R. But what about within the church?

S. Within the church, I think, yes. And I think if we could be careful to get the function before we get the title, then I think we will be okay.

I've been contacted several times by people who want me to be an apostolic organization, or something. And they said, "Well, you're functioning that way." But I didn't join them or anything like that. Paul said, "If I'm not an apostle to them, at least I am to you." I know that hundreds and hundreds of people consider me to be an apostle. But I'm comfortable enough; I don't need a title. I function at it and I love the function.

I'd like to see a little more of the function of a true prophet among us. I think that part of the problem with that is—just as you are trying to define better in your book what revival is, where we've gone wrong, where we've gone right—I think we need prophets better functioning in our churches. So many of the prophets that I've dealt with, or people who said they had a prophetic ministry—when I listen to their prophecy, they are basically chirping what anybody could say—even what my granddaughter could say: "God loves you, you're going to have a big ministry, and your future looks bright."

R. That would not be a seasoned prophet as I would recognize one.

S. And I want the seasoned prophet.

R. Someone like Agabus of the Bible.

S. I have seasoned prophets here that nobody in the world recognizes as prophets. They don't care if they have the title of a prophet. But when they come up as prayer warriors and pray for you, you'll do what the woman at the well did. She left and said, "Come see a man who told me all that I am." They will tell you who you are right then and there.

This means, if God does reveal who you are right then, in my opinion, that means He's willing to do something about it right then. It's a striking moment—a prophetic moment—the old phrase applies, "They read my mail." But it's not a public, "Thus sayeth the Lord, I'm reading your mail." It's done, bang, bang!

I'd just like to see a little more of the true prophetic announcement come out about this revival. And I believe I could do that if I pressed it a little harder, but, for some reason, I've never felt the comfort zone that that's what I'm supposed to be doing.

R. But it sounds like you're trying to incorporate all of those gifts and release them in your church.

S. Absolutely. I would love to. I want more true evangelists among us. I don't want to get up and be the evangelist. I just want them every week to be so burning up with evangelism that they're always saying, "You guys need to get out there." I want them within the congregation. I have them, but I want more evangelists and their abilities more fined-tuned.

R. The other night Roy Fields mentioned that your message on revival worship moved him deeply. Do you have some things you might want to add about that?

S. Oh, yeah. You have all these worship leaders and he's one of them who's been doing it and doing it and doing it. And, there again, there are a lot of preconceived ideas—I've spent a lot of years being in this and new ones come along and pick up a little bit here and there, but basically it was the Word of God that did it.

It's like I said, in many revivals the Word of God is pretty weak. But I've kept it a primary thing in my own life. Maybe I can thank Kenneth Copeland for that—and people like that who emphasized the Word, the Word, the Word. And I've done a lot of studies.

Marketers today have found out that the strongest way to influence people to buy things, and get the money out of them is to explain the "why." However, so much of the time we explain the "what," and we don't explain the "why." I think even Roy, as a worship leader all these years, knows the "what"—so he's preaching the "what"—this is *what* we do—but it becomes weak because they say, "Okay, let's all raise our hands and worship the Lord," and half the people do and half the people don't. Worship leaders can't convince them why they should. They just know it looks good, I guess. What I did was to give them the "why" on different levels.

At the end of it I shared with them the "why"—what makes me "tick." I shared with them that, for me, it made no sense that I should be here on this earth at all. I would ask, "Why am I here? Why am I a Christian?" And I would get all these answers like, "God created you because He was lonely. You need to get saved so you can go to heaven and be with God. God created you so that you can die and go to heaven." All these answers were floating around.

To me it made no sense, because I thought, "Why couldn't you just create me as an angel and leave me up in heaven where it's safe?" Down here it's a little risky. The devil's here; hell could be knocking at your door, if you don't do it right. Some people are going to go to heaven and some people are going to go to hell. This seems like a big risk. It made no sense to me to put me even close to where the devil was working.

So I began to develop this idea, and I began to realize that so many of my thought patterns were about me and trying to figure out why I'm here. I was looking at the events that happened in my life, never about the events that happened in the Kingdom of God and taking them seriously.

I realized that when Satan led his rebellion and took one third of the angels with him—when he rose up in pride—that he also accused God—and still does—and he convinced these angels that he was right. And out they went.

I never stood there in the Spirit with God and watched them leave. I never did that. I acted like it was a small event. "Here, God, what do you care, you've got lots of angels." I never took it seriously—this serious event. Yet, as a pastor, when people would leave my church, I wanted everybody to sympathize with me. Well, it's heartbreaking. I raised these people, I preached, and now they are gone. I felt bad, but I never felt it for God. So I began to examine it and said, "Wait a minute, this was a crushing, embarrassing, shameful thing that happened."

So I started realizing that maybe that's it. I wasn't placed here as an afterthought, or because God's lonely, or because He brought me here because he wants to get me saved. In fact, if God wanted me in heaven, why didn't He just create me there? He created me here and then I go to heaven and then what happens to me? According to the Bible, I turn right back around and come back here again. What is going on?

Then I thought, "You know what? I'm planted here for a reason. The reason is that when that huge event happened in heaven—that's one of the major heavenly events that are recorded—it was such a shameful moment that God was dishonored.

The only thing that God cannot have or get for himself (and there is only one thing that I can think of) is He risks me. I could be here doing something—I could follow Satan; I could follow God. But I've chosen to follow God. I've chosen to worship Him. I've chosen to preach His way. And I've chosen to say how good He is. God can't do that Himself because the second He does, it's not honorable anymore.

After this revelation, I got the dads, moms, and kids together at church and said, "Listen, what could we do to restore God's honor? We looked down the row and saw Barbies, GI Joes, coloring books, doodlers and we thought, "You know what, we could probably do better than that." I said, "Dad, let's talk to the kids and say, 'You know, kids, God's got everything. If we could get His honor back, then we could get more from Him. What do you say we put these toys away and we try to give God the only thing He can't have?'" And you know what, the kids understood it! We'll be more blessed as a result.

So I used the example of the guy who came at midnight trying to get more bread, pounding on the door. I studied that through and there were key words like "importunity," then "boldness," then "persistence," and then I got down to the bottom and there was "because of his shamelessness."

We translate this into English, "he shamefully kept pounding." Then I studied the culture and it wasn't that at all. The actual line was, "In order to prevent shame, he got up." Not because he was a friend. He didn't give him bread because he was a friend, but in order to prevent shame. Then I realized—then the culture came in and I realized that if a man came in from out of town and needed bread and the community didn't give him any, then the others in the community would say, "Well, shame on you!"

So what made the guy get out of bed at midnight and give him bread? It wasn't because he was a friend. It was in order to prevent shame from coming on the community, so he gave him as much as he needed.

I told them that and I said, "If we could help prevent more shame, God will get out of bed and we can have as much bread as we want. So let's tell our kids if they will help me with this, then we'll get more bread. He's going to get out of bed and give us more bread. But we're also going to prevent more shame. So let's put all the toys away. What would it hurt us to lift our hands? We could do that. We could do that."

All of a sudden the "why" came in, and you weren't just telling people, "Get up your hands." And you didn't have the idea, "Well, my church just doesn't do that. And Steve Gray, he tells us to do that, but my church doesn't do that." Once the "why" came in you get the anointing and the stories, and all that with it. Roy said three times this wave of tears just came. "I got it. After all these years, I got it. I know why I'm supposed to do this. I have something that only I can give to God."

So this has motivated our people. They show up to honor God. That's a powerful revival! That's revival. I mean, if you show up to honor God, that's revival. It may not have signs and wonders, or be as explosive as you think and visitors might not come. But that's revival. You have revived something—and God comes near you because you're giving God the one thing He can't give Himself. It's really powerful.

R. Well, excellent.

S. So just little jewels like that over all these years—I go into a church or into a ministry or speak to my own people, and just give them these little jewels. And you show them the "why," then you create hunger in them, and they do the rest of the work. That's my technique, at least, to maintain it.

So I've been able to do it. Revival is burning just as hot as ever and just as life changing. You have a person of God that's been struggling and hurting, and suddenly their hope has been renewed and they are ready to go back out. And they love Jesus. This is revival, too—you love God more than you did a few minutes before. You've been revived.

So it's on different levels, but that's what I do anyway.

R. Thank you, Steve.

9

Dr. Michael Brown

Teacher and Revivalist
November 12, 2011

Dr. Michael Brown served as a leader in the Brownsville revival from 1996-2000, and was founder and president of the Brownsville Revival School of Ministry (1997-2000), out of which was birthed FIRE School of Ministry (2001-present). From the summer of 1996 through 2000, Dr. Brown taught day sessions at the revival for leaders (on Fridays) and the general public (on Saturdays), participated in all the night services every week, and was one of the speakers in the revival's Awake America campaigns across the nation, as well as in the Awake Germany and Awake Singapore campaigns.

Currently, Dr. Brown is the founder and president of FIRE School of Ministry in Concord, North Carolina, director of the Coalition of Conscience, and host of the daily, nationally, syndicated talk radio show, "The Line of Fire," as well as the host of the Jewish-outreach, documentary TV series, "Think It Thru."

ꕤ ꕤ

Michael Brown graciously met me at his ministry offices with a mustached smile and a big handshake. His office looked like a miniature library with reference books, commentaries, and Bibles covering every possible spot—wall-to-wall and floor to ceiling. (Here is a man after my heart!) A large microphone stood in front of his desk from which he broadcasts his radio show.

He walked me around the ministry offices a bit while talking about his students and missionaries to India. We found a quiet spot where we slid into some chairs. You could tell revival was on his heart.

The Interview

Michael: This is the fortieth anniversary of when I first believed in Jesus—although it took about five weeks for me to surrender. But this was the first time I actually believed that this was real.

Randy: Outstanding! Wow! For me, it's been quite a long time. I think I was about ten years old when I went through a confirmation class—or something like that.

I just want to start off with a question in general. *Tell me what revival means to you and what are your thoughts about revival in general?*

M. From a technical level, revival is a season of unusual, divine visitation. That's the long and short of it. And it results in certain things because God comes in an unusually intense way. So there is deep conviction; there is powerful repentance; there is radical returning to God; there is radical salvation. But it's basically a fresh encounter with God. It's renewal of "first love." As Finney said, it's a new beginning of obedience to the Lord—the return of the Church from her backslidings. So it begins with the people of God but then it spreads out and touches the world.

When you think of it on a less tactical level, you're just experiencing the overwhelming goodness and love and grace, power and purity of God—either for the first time, or, in most cases, once again. And it's absolutely, radically, life transforming. And it's that which is absolutely needed to get the Church back to where it needs to be, because we tend to backslide or get in ruts or get beaten down or become worldly or compromising and don't even know it. Revival is that which has to get us back to where we need to be—revived. The goal, of course, is to sustain it.

R. Let me ask you another question about Leonard Ravenhill. I think I heard once that you had known him—that he was a revivalist. How did his ministry touch your life?

M. We were very close the last five years of his life. And that had a profound effect on me. But the impact began earlier. I was saved in 1971—radically committed to Jesus. By the time I was saved for a year, I would spend six hours alone with God in the Word and prayer every day—memorizing twenty verses a day—full of zeal and passion.

By the time I was saved ten or eleven years—I was getting my PhD—I had allowed intellectualism and theological pride to get in the way of my passion. I was still very much committed to the Lord, but had really drifted from my "first love" on a serious level—although I thought I had just matured.

In 1982, God began to bring me through a time of repentance and returning to the passion and fervor and commitment that I once had. During that season—late '82 and early '83—where we actually had an outpouring of the Spirit; God got a hold of me. It was in a traditional church. The Holy Spirit fell upon me and touched many in the church.

Many of us started reading Leonard Ravenhill books—*Why Revival Tarries* and *Revival Praying* were the first ones that we read. To this day I still quote from some of the quotes from the leaders that are in the beginning of each chapter in those books.

In April of '83—this is after we had the outpouring in our church for about three months, and, ultimately, the Spirit was quenched and resisted and leaders divided over what God was doing—we went to hear Leonard speak at Brooklyn Tabernacle. At that time he was about 76 years old.

He brought a message on Samson. And it was one of the most convicting messages I'd ever heard in my life. I just felt the Spirit's presence powerfully in the midst of this deep conviction. When he gave an altar call—just for people to cry out to the Lord and pray for the pastor and seek God—the altars were flooded by people weeping and wailing. We looked at each other and thought, "This is what we were experiencing at the *height* of the outpouring in our church and this is just following him as he preaches!"

Six years later, when I wrote my first book on revival, *The End of the American Gospel Enterprise*, God impressed on me that Leonard would write the foreword to my book. Even though I wasn't sure that he was even alive.

I happened to meet his son, David, preaching in Kansas City, asked him about his dad, got his address, wrote him a letter, but didn't ask Bro. Len for anything, except for comments and criticisms, because I was sure he was going to write the foreword. In fact, I had already told the publisher that he would be writing the foreword, even though we had never formally met. He got the manuscript and immediately volunteered to write the foreword to the book, and then embraced me as a spiritual son and a friend.

During the last five years of his life, we were in regular contact. A couple of times a year I would just go down and spend a few days with him—pray together, talk—we talked by phone constantly. He would send me things he wanted me to read.

He was definitely the most broken-hearted man of God I've ever met. The overwhelming burden that he carried [was remarkable]. I'd be with him in his home and he'd come out from one of his prayer times with this look of shock on his face, "Mike, the Church is naked!" Every day was the same, as if it was the first time he had seen it. He carried such a burden for the state of the Bride, and he was very intimate with Jesus. And yet, when he would minister, even in his eighties—I was in meetings where he couldn't even finish his preaching because the whole place was filled with people weeping and wailing and crying out to God. He couldn't even finish his message.

So I saw the effects of his prayer life even when he was frail. I had been fully-formed in my burden for revival at that point—my passion, my belief in the power of repentance—those things were formed in me and that's what brought us our union—but he poured fuel on that fire. He deepened it. He helped deepen the spiritual roots in my life.

He introduced me to the writings of Catherine Booth, for example. He also introduced Keith Green to those things. [He introduced me to] some of the Puritans I hadn't read as much—just added further fuel to my fire and confirmed me in the direction I was going. And I believe that his prayers for me on a regular basis helped me in that season of writing—when I wrote *End of the American Gospel Enterprise* and *How Saved Are We?* and *Whatever Happened to the Power of God?* and some other books.

Actually, that was the connection to Steve Hill and Brownsville, ultimately. Steve was also close with Bro. Len. When Steve moved back from Argentina, Len gave him one of my books, *Our Hands Are Stained with Blood*, a book about the Church and the Jewish people. Then Steve connected with me and asked me to endorse something that he had written. Then I began to recognize the spiritual heritage in Steve's life. So when revival broke in Brownsville, and I heard that Steve was in the middle of it, I knew that this must be the real thing, because of his burden for the lost and his belief in holiness and his preaching of repentance.

Len had gone to be with the Lord at that point—November of '94 at the age of 87. So that was some months before Brownsville. But here it unfolds that two of the principle people allowed to serve in the midst of that revival were people he was very close to and poured his life into. I don't doubt that his prayers—his tears—helped birth what happened there.

R. That's marvelous. So what do you think brings revival and what hinders it?

M. The old question, "Why don't we have revival?" still has the old answer, "Because we are willing to live without it." God can move in ways that we don't understand and through people who are not likely in settings that don't make sense to us. Let God be God.

But in terms of what we do know, if we are preparing the way, He responds to hunger and thirst. You can have rain on concrete, and it doesn't go anywhere. You can have that same rain on parched ground and it drinks it in. Jesus is born in a manger because there is no room in the inn. Laodicea said, "I am rich, increased in wealth, and have need of nothing." It didn't realize that it was wretched, pitiful, poor, blind, and naked. The churches Jesus commends in Revelation—like Smyrna—[are those for which He says,] "I know your poverty and your afflictions, but I know you are rich." Those of us who think we have it all together—"We're doing just great—the church is wonderful—we've never been more successful"—and perhaps we are experiencing some of God's blessings, but we won't be candidates for revival. We wouldn't welcome the move—we wouldn't welcome God and the intensity and the soul-searching and the disruption of our lives and schedules.

So revival comes in response to desperation—to hunger and thirst—that we just have to have God. It can come because we are personally desperate—we can't live the way we've been living. Either we see sin in our own lives or we're living for God and that living for Him makes us hungrier and thirstier. It can be the needs of the world around us and we have no answer for them. It can be the recognition of the backslidden state of the Church in general. But either way it's something that gets us to that point of hunger and thirst.

There are many promises in the Word to the hungry and thirsty. There are not any to the full and satisfied—that are positive, anyway. Jesus said, "Blessed are those who hunger and thirst for righteousness, they'll be filled." Jesus said, "If anyone is thirsty, let him come unto me and drink." That's the pre-requisite—a hunger and thirst—a recognition that something is wrong—the recognition that this is not the way it's supposed to be. Either from what the Word speaks, either from the hunger of our own heart, either from what God has done in history—we say this cannot be the way it's supposed to be. This cannot be all that God has for His people. There must be more.

Then seek God until the answer comes. And be willing to let God do what He wants to do regardless of cost or consequence. As long as we have our little program within which God has to fit, we'll never see revival. As long as personal reputation or the status quo is more important, we'll never have revival. But when we are so hungry and thirsty that we cannot live without His blessing, then we can see Him move. And when He comes, we'll see the move continue.

R. When your heart is matted down and hard, like that concrete surface you were talking about, what do you do to begin to break up that ground? What prayers do you ask? Do you ask for God's grace to help you to be hungry and thirsty?

M. You have to start where you are. You can't manufacture something. I know in 1982, as God began to convict me about my intellectual and theological pride and my mistaking coldness for maturity, that I said to myself, "I can make a radical shift that will last for a few days and that will be it. What can I do? I have to turn in the right direction. If I'm praying five minutes in a day, I'll pray ten. If I'm praying fifteen, I'll pray a half hour. If I'm not praying at all, I'll pray ten minutes—just start going in the direction I have to go."

For sure, if we find ourselves in the position of having to break up the fallow ground, we have to make efforts. And we are able to make the effort; God will help us. It may just be pleading with God for a breakthrough, because we realize we can't break through. "God, demonstrate the power of the Spirit in my life. Demonstrate that Jesus is risen from the dead in my own life."

It can be about appealing to God for His name's sake and for His glory. It's also very healthy to read things—just be reading more in the Word about these things. And do things differently. Get on your knees and open the Bible and read out loud and ask God to speak to you. "Lord, change me as I'm reading this." Read other accounts of revival. Read things that get you hungry and thirsty.

If you've been in ministry yourself, and there were times when you were really passionate—maybe you've got an old message on a CD or a tape—maybe you've written something when you were at the height of passion—go back and read it. Let your own words, your own writings convict you. If you journal, and there were times of really walking in intimacy and a tremendous prayer life—go back and read—read things that will make you jealous. Read things that will convict you. Listen to things that will make you realize how far you've fallen—not to condemn you, but to get you to a point where you are crying out. And then, little by little, or quite suddenly, God can answer.

R. Amen. Good advice. What do you think really hinders revival? Or anything uniquely today that is hindering it?

M. Big question. Let me speak generically, then specifically, to that. Generically, lack of hunger, lack of spiritual honesty, having to own the thing or control it, also ignorance of who God really is and what He really wants to do, so you think your situation is it, because that's all you've ever known.

To give you an extreme example, if you've grown up in a racist family, then you think that racism or racist culture is normal. So we grow up in certain church cultures and think, "This is it. This is what church is." And we read the Word through that lens.

Also, a theology that says, "It's over. It's too late. It's all coming down. There'll be no more revival. America has gone too far. The end-time clock is ticking and we are past the time of revival." Or wrong theology that says, "There can be no more revival." And then personal discouragement, hopelessness, "God may move somewhere else, but He's not going to work through me. I've disqualified myself. I've fallen one too many times. I've been too prayerless. I've had the opportunity. I blew it." Self-condemnation—those kinds of things can always get in the way.

In our contemporary culture, so much of the Church is in such a state of deception in regards to the nature of the gospel. We have so watered things down. It is so much an "all about me" message. There's so little preaching of the cross. The idea of conviction of sin is foreign in many circles. We have brought the message down to accommodate people. "God exists to satisfy my dreams and help me to reach my personal goals." These are some of the wrong concepts we have in the Body. We have focused far more on being relevant than on being right with God. And thus, have made ourselves irrelevant.

So we are in a state today, especially with the younger generation, of extreme biblical illiteracy, with a very low biblical worldview throughout the church, with a very low conception of who God is, and very little fear or reverence of God. And much of this emphasis on His power is somewhat superficial—not really an encounter that can change my life, but something exciting that changes the things around me.

So because of that, we have drifted to a point where we don't even realize how deeply we have drifted. If the norm is I'm supposed to weigh 500 pounds and I weigh 490, then I'm in good shape. If the norm is that I should weigh 150 pounds, and I weigh 500, then I'm near death. We have drifted from so many fundamentals. Things are up for grabs now, doctrinally, that weren't even discussed as possibilities, except by the cults a generation ago.

And those that hold to biblical authority or biblical values are now considered fanatical and extremists. Because of that, there's hardly even recognition of the need for visitation, outpouring, or revival. And it becomes a much larger picture, because, with revival, there needs to be restoration of so many biblical truths. It can't just be God reviving something that has gotten dry. There needs to be a complete revamping—even a revolution in many, many ways.

R. Then what sustains revival?

M. On the one hand the prayer that helps birth it is essential to sustain it. The hunger needs to continue. You don't want to get complacent in the midst of it. There must be a continual pouring out—the principle of give and it shall be given you remains.

One of the strengths of Brownsville was that we had a tremendous passion for the lost. It was in our hearts, and then, of course, Steve was the "igniter" of that with his extraordinary evangelistic burden. The school had a tremendous burden for the lost and for world missions. That's why, to this day, we have our grads that we work with serving the Lord all over the world, bearing much fruit. And that hunger continues in our midst. It's a part of who we are.

So when God's touching you and you now pour that out—when God's blessing you and you're not just soaking it in—you're not getting so fat you can't even get out the church doors—you're rejoicing in His goodness but also looking to touch a dying and hurting world, of course it's going to allow for the flow to continue.

When we were ministering night in and night out—it was a very exhausting pace—my schedule was often 80 to 100 hours a week of ministry-related activity. You would often be at the point of exhaustion. But, the recognition that this was something you've been longing for for years and years—for your whole life—you don't know how long it's going to last. The recognition that people were coming hungry and thirsty from around the world wanting a touch from God—and the recognition that when you ministered to them something supernatural was happening—that was a sustaining force as well.

So the seizing the moment, and then the hunger of others and then the fruit of the ministry—is the cycle of ongoing life. Obviously, keeping the vessels pure, staying low because "God resists the proud, but gives grace to the humble"—if we allow sin—be it sexual sin or monetary sin, or pride or other things like that—to pollute, that will stop things. We're not earning [revival], but we are just keeping our vessels pure so that God doesn't get grieved and have to withdraw. You want an environment where He feels at home.

To the extent that you avoid the "superstar" mentality and continue to exalt Jesus, is essential. Those working together need to have solid relationships. Often, that's a challenge in the midst of everything that's happening and the intensity of schedule.

To the extent that there's relational harmony—that's important for the Holy Spirit to feel at home. The anointing on Aaron—it says in Psalm 133, "brothers dwelling together in unity"—that's the ideal picture.

Before Brownsville, as I sensed that there was refreshing happening in many circles, I was encouraged by some reports I had heard. I had some concerns, but I had no question that something was happening. I began to preach that to go from refreshing to real revival—where there would not just be blessing and renewal, but repentance, transformation and even touching the world—there were two ditches on either side of the road. There was the ditch of religious traditionalism—"We've never done this like this before. This is different. This is challenging our authority structure or our power base or denominational heritage"—whatever it is.

Then, on the opposite side, was another ditch that I would describe as superficial sensationalism, or manifestation mania.

You get so caught up with the stuff that happened that you completely lose sight of why you were praying for the outpouring in the first place. These two ditches on either side would then intensify. The one would call the other "Pharisees." The other would say, "This is the devil," and they would get further and further apart.

Before Brownsville, I was preaching that what we have to do is keep our eyes focused on Jesus, be open to the Holy Spirit, but put our entire emphasis on holiness and harvest—holiness in the Church, harvest in the world—a message of repentance to the Church and a message of repentance to the world.

If we do that, we will avoid the ditches on either side of the road and we could really go from refreshing to revival. That's what I saw as paramount within Brownsville: Jesus being exalted, freedom in the Holy Spirit—"God move however you want to move, whatever the cost or consequence, if it's genuinely you, we embrace it"—and then an emphasis on holiness in the Church and harvest in the world. To me, the life flow will then, continue.

Of course, you cannot sustain the intensity of revival in its full heat year after year after year. It's not even practical for a local church [to do that]. But somehow that visitation has to become a habitation. So there has to be a revival culture—a church that reflects this—so that you don't need a revival five or ten to twenty years later. At least that's the goal.

R. That's some really good insight. One of the things that I observed from a distance at Brownsville—I visited there a few times—actually, you prayed for me one time with all the multitudes you prayed for—I felt like you had an evangelist, a teacher, and a pastor there. When I look at Ephesians 4:11—there is a desire to include all the gift ministries to bring the saints to maturity. I consider yourself a teacher, and yet you probably have strong leanings toward evangelism and revival, too. Then John Kilpatrick was more of a pastor and Steve was an evangelist. That was providing a real balance in ministry there. *Have you given any thought to that kind of thing as it was transpiring?*

M. We certainly recognized the different gifts and anointing. What's interesting is that I'm not an evangelist as Steve is, in terms of just that focus of winning the lost. I do evangelistic work all the time—share my faith. And to the Jewish people I'm a strong evangelist. But, when I go to India, for example, they're not expecting me to do evangelistic meetings. They want me to equip the saints—to bring a prophetic message to the Church. So most of the years while traveling, my burden was a prophetic wake-up call to the Body and revival flowing out of that. My teaching role was more in a school setting.

When I got to Brownsville, it was necessary for me to "wear a different hat." I was not primarily preaching; I was teaching. I was giving theological foundations to what was happening. I was used to being the keynote speaker wherever I was at conferences. Now I was supporting Steve every night, and we knew that was absolutely right. I looked forward to it. I loved it. I was never bored. So we each recognized that everyone had a role.

What we had to do on the school setting was to be sure that we built other components in, as opposed to primarily building on an evangelistic ministry, because of the thrust of the revival. We needed to be more intentionally, holistically five-fold on the school so that the students would be trained beyond just a revival setting.

For me, what I would minister at the leader's meetings was a very strong prophetic message—at the semi-annual pastor's conferences that we had a Brownsville. The messages would be very sharp and very prophetic messages to the Church because I was functioning in a different setting then. But in the revival week to week it was in a different, supportive function.

Ultimately, for multiplication purposes and things like that, to the extent that you have the five-fold ministries covered, that's wonderful. John Kilpatrick gave most of the pastoral duties over to others as the revival intensified and continued. He was stepping out more and more into things on a national level. And on a certain level, we recognized that part of the reason we need revival has to do with our Church "wineskins" and our way of doing things—and I say "our" meaning any of us. I'm sure there are inherited ways in all of us that get in the way of God's best.

As God moves in revival, He wants to change a lot of things. In other words, He doesn't just want to impart His blessing within a certain wineskin. Perhaps the wineskin needs adjusting. Perhaps we need to revisit some of the things we believe and hold to. Maybe that was part of our issue.

I believe there were many looking to Brownsville for almost a new paradigm, or model. We had begun to birth something as spiritual fathers to our students—ordaining them and sending them. And they were going out and planting new works. But at that time it brought a degree of conflict with some of the other brothers that we were working with because their structure was different.

It wasn't a matter of right versus wrong. It was simply a matter of one thing that was more of a centralized headquarters approach and the other that was more organic and fathering. For us, that was an apostolic model that could have grown, but we didn't get to live that out together. Allowing more fathering and organic reproduction—laying hands on your spiritual sons and sending them out—could have been a new paradigm and is at the heart of being apostolic.

In its fullest sense, for revival to reach its goal, there has to be a rethinking or changing of some of the wineskins. And I don't mean that it has to be house churches or it can't be denominational. I'm not making sweeping statements as much as I'm saying we can't just assume that the structure is sound and that God wants to pour out His Spirit within that. But sometimes there needs to be more fundamental restructuring and that's part of what effective five-fold ministry is all about.

R. I agree with you. What are some of the most important lessons you've learned about revival.

M. First, is that true revival is everything it's cracked up to be. Many times when we talk about it, I just break down crying because of the reality of the things we've seen the Lord do. I've seen the Lord do many wonderful things over the years and many wonderful things to this day, but there was an extraordinary season of several years and some seasons of months at other times before and after Brownsville that were extraordinary. But revival is everything it's cracked up to be—the depth of the encounter with God, the song of joy getting put back into your heart, the reality of who He is. There is nothing more valuable. There is nothing more wonderful.

Another important lesson would be to become even more jealous when God does move, and to be willing to rearrange things and to look with foresight to see how this can be sustained. You just don't know how many times in your life, or in a century, when you will be exposed to God moving in those ways.

I had started to write a book towards the end of my time at Brownsville on *25 Sure-fire Ways to Put Out the Spirit's Fire*. I still do plan to finish the book. I believe it will be relevant again in many ways as God moves afresh. But, whatever can be done to avoid exhaustion, whatever can be done to deepen personal relationships, whatever can be done to help others look beyond the excitement of the moment—these are very important.

I would also say that revival confirmed so many things that I had preached and believed for years and years. While I'm always open to God moving in some other way and I never want to be the guy who says, "This can't be the Lord because it's different from what I'm used to," I still don't believe you're ever going to get far away from the foundations of real repentance and deep conviction of sin producing lasting change. The message may come differently, but if it doesn't bring deep repentance, a deep transformation of life, and believers walking in the beauty of holiness, I don't care what you call it, it's not revival.

Meat and potatoes—the basics—majoring on the majors, these are all important—teach, equip, strengthen others. The main thrust has to be the main thrust and, if we deviate from that, we'll quickly become a sideshow.

R. Do you have any thoughts about some of the revivals that have taken place recently in America other than Brownsville?

M. I continue to be encouraged by the prayer movement and the houses of prayer. A number of our grads are involved with different houses of prayer in different parts of the country or in Kansas City. So many people, especially young people, are gravitating to deep worship of Jesus and much prayer and intercession. To me, that's a very encouraging sign in the midst of a lot of youth apostasy.

Also, any time there is a move that centers on one person and the one person is young and doesn't have the best track record of stability in history, you can almost guarantee that it's coming down quickly. To the extent that there is a team, to the extent that we avoid the "superstar" status, to the extent that we stay centered in Scripture and not get involved in esoteric doctrines, to the extent that we put personal morality and holiness and solid family life ahead of gifting, to that extent we have a better chance of sustainability. There is a real devil who wants to take people out.

There was one recent move that was taking place—I prayed for God to work, I did my best to be a positive encouragement, as opposed to being a negative gainsayer. The Lord made clear to me that I was to keep my mouth shut and say nothing, but I wrote in my journal, "This is an accident waiting to happen."

Again, you had the ingredients of one person suddenly exalted, of very little preaching of the Word, of sometimes more exaltation of angels and esoteric things than of Jesus Himself, and lack of team in ministry. And because of that, you could be relatively sure that the enemy was going to come in and destroy this pretty quickly. Or it would just implode—one way or another.

I'm blessed, however, by some other things happening in the Body—outpouring of the Spirit, greater healing and people sustaining a first-love in a beautiful and wonderful way. I get concerned, though, when the preaching of holiness and the preaching of repentance becomes an "enemy." I know there is legalism out there. I know there are people beating others over the head. But, when we don't embrace the beauty of holiness, and when we don't embrace the beauty of the message of repentance, something is already amiss.

R. Holiness and the presence of God are inseparable things.

M. Yes, exactly. So I get concerned when all preaching of holiness is branded legalism, when quoting of Scripture is called "the letter," and when reverence for God is called "dead religion." Those things deeply concern me. To me, it means already something is off track and will go further off track.

Any movement that puts its primary emphasis on healings and miracles and does not emphasize character, transformation of life, and reaching the lost, is already off. Although we want to see a demonstration of God's power, I know there is still far more that God wants to do.

I would also say that any revival movement that does not end up with a very strong burden to touch society is missing something, because we are called to be the moral conscience of society. If we just divorce ourselves and thank God for His blessings while society goes to hell, then something, again, is missing.

R. I agree. Thank you. Thank you very much.

10

The Culture of Revival

"Somehow visitation has to become a habitation.
So there has to be a revival culture
—a church that reflects this."
—Dr. Michael Brown

The Journey

After those 88 days of revival at our church, I began a three-year journey to discover what we can do to sustain revival—to make it a part of our culture—and to write this book. That journey led me to interview several of the revival "giants" and glean from them the principles of sustaining revival.

The task before us is to try to gather these principles together and make some sense out of the remarkable advice these men and women of God have shared with us and develop a strategy for revival. To that end, I offer the following highlights:

1. *Lay the groundwork with the most important ingredients to revival and keep them burning: prayer, conviction, confession, and repentance.* Conviction and repentance need to do their ever-deepening work. Confession of sin should come from an appreciation for the beauty of holiness.

   Pray revival. Preach revival. Talk revival. Never stop doing the things that brought revival. If the people lose the spirit of prayer, the revival will end. In contrast, an army of dedicated intercessors will sustain revival.

2. *Pastor the revival and maintain its rhythms.* The leadership must have the courage to guide the congregation in the Spirit and do whatever is necessary to prevent offending Him.

   There are many times the members must be encouraged and given hope (e.g. the "height" of revival). At other times the congregants must be broken down and made to realize their sinfulness (e.g. the "depth" of revival). As Steve Gray put it in a spiritual equation, "height plus depth equals length."

   Hunger and humility are necessary ingredients for God's continued blessings. Apathy and pride will bring an abrupt end to any revival. If the congregation ever loses its "exquisite relish for Divine things" (Finney), the revival will end.

3. *Minister in one accord and make every effort to release all the gift ministries.*

   The leaders must minister in unity. If any are willing to live without revival—if any lose their desperation for revival— the result will be disunity and, ultimately, an end to the revival.

   The leaders must major on the important things and not let the revival become a "sideshow." They must also be men and women of the Word of God and never compromise its importance.

   They must also organize volunteers to maintain the administration of the revival and prevent exhaustion in the leadership. However, all who minister must have a continual willingness to be poured out as a sacrifice to God.

   God designed the church with multifaceted gift-ministries and these need to be recognized for their respective contributions and released to minister during revival.

4. *Recognize any new "wineskin" needed for revival.* A revival-based church is not your "seeker-sensitive," program-based, one-man centered, entertainment-oriented church that permeates church culture in America today.

   Presence-based churches seek first to allow the Holy Spirit to have His way in the service. And the members of these churches must strike a balance between church traditions and "superficial sensationalism."

5. *Carry the gospel to the community.* If we are satisfied with soaking in the glory alone, the revival will end. Ultimately, our prayers must turn into tears for lost souls.

In the final chapter of Steve Gray's book, *My Absurd Religion*, he describes the kind of desperation-prayer that it takes to bring revival. He discovered it one evening as he rushed to the hospital to pray with the parents of a child who had just been in a terrible accident. Desperation-prayer for revival is like the plea for God from parents who are crying out for their child as they wait outside the ER. This type of desperation-prayer was the turning point for Pastor Steve and it will do the same for you.

Are you willing to live without revival?